YOUR
AUTHORITY
IN CHRIST

STUDY **7**

YOUR AUTHORITY
IN CHRIST

OVERCOME STRONGHOLDS IN YOUR LIFE

NEIL T. ANDERSON

BETHANYHOUSE
a division of Baker Publishing Group
www.BethanyHouse.com

© 2015 by Neil T. Anderson

Published by Bethany House Publishers
11400 Hampshire Avenue South
Bloomington, Minnesota 55438
www.bethanyhouse.com

Bethany House Publishers is a division of
Baker Publishing Group, Grand Rapids, Michigan

Printed in the United States of America

Library of Congress Control Number: 2014958632

ISBN 978-0-7642-1704-3

Unless otherwise indicated, Scripture quotations are from the Holy Bible, New International Version®. NIV®. Copyright © 1973, 1978, 1984, 2011 by Biblica, Inc.™ Used by permission of Zondervan. All rights reserved worldwide. www.zondervan.com

Scripture quotations identified NASB are from the New American Standard Bible®, copyright © 1960, 1962, 1963, 1968, 1971, 1972, 1973, 1975, 1977, 1995 by The Lockman Foundation. Used by permission.

Scripture quotations identified KJV are from the King James Version of the Bible.

Cover design by Rob Williams, InsideOutCreativeArts

15   16   17   18   19   20   21   7   6   5   4   3   2   1

Contents

Contents

Introduction

The Victory Series

S o then, just as you received Christ Jesus as Lord, continue to live your lives in him, rooted and built up in him, strengthened in the faith as you were taught" (Colossians 2:6–7). Paul's New Covenant theology is based on who we are "in Christ." As a believer in Christ, you must first be rooted "in Him" so you can be built up "in Him." Just as you encounter challenges as you grow physically, you will encounter hurdles as you grow spiritually. The following chart illustrates what obstacles you need to overcome and lessons you need to learn at various stages of growth spiritually, rationally, emotionally, volitionally, and relationally.

Levels of Conflict

	Level One Rooted in Christ	Level Two Built up in Christ	Level Three Living in Christ
Spiritual	Lack of salvation or assurance (Eph. 2:1–3)	Living according to the flesh (Gal. 5:19–21)	Insensitive to the Spirit's leading (Heb. 5:11–14)
Rational	Pride and ignorance (1 Cor. 8:1)	Wrong belief or philosophy (Col. 2:8)	Lack of knowledge (Hos. 4:6)
Emotional	Fearful, guilty, and shameful (Matt. 10:26–33; Rom. 3:23)	Angry, anxious, and depressed (Eph. 4:31; 1 Pet. 5:7; 2 Cor. 4:1–18)	Discouraged and sorrowful (Gal. 6:9)

	Level One Rooted in Christ	**Level Two** Built up in Christ	**Level Three** Living in Christ
Volitional	Rebellious (1 Tim. 1:9)	Lack of self-control (1 Cor. 3:1–3)	Undisciplined (2 Thess. 3:7, 11)
Relational	Rejected and unloved (1 Pet. 2:4)	Bitter and unforgiving (Col. 3:13)	Selfish (1 Cor. 10:24; Phil. 2:1–5)

This VICTORY SERIES will address these obstacles and hurdles and help you understand what it means to be firmly rooted in Christ, grow in Christ, live free in Christ, and overcome in Christ. The goal of the course is to help you attain greater levels of spiritual growth, as the following diagram illustrates:

Levels of Growth

	Level One Rooted in Christ	**Level Two** Built up in Christ	**Level Three** Living in Christ
Spiritual	Child of God (Rom. 8:16)	Lives according to the Spirit (Gal. 5:22–23)	Led by the Spirit (Rom. 8:14)
Rational	Knows the truth (John 8:32)	Correctly uses the Bible (2 Tim. 2:15)	Adequate and equipped (2 Tim. 3:16–17)
Emotional	Free (Gal. 5:1)	Joyful, peaceful, and patient (Gal. 5:22)	Contented (Phil. 4:11)
Volitional	Submissive (Rom. 13:1–5)	Self-controlled (Gal. 5:23)	Disciplined (1 Tim. 4:7–8)
Relational	Accepted and forgiven (Rom. 5:8; 15:7)	Forgiving (Eph. 4:32)	Loving and unselfish (Phil. 2:1–5)

God's Story for You and *Your New Identity*, the first two studies in the VICTORY SERIES, focused on the issues that help the believer become firmly rooted in Christ (level one in above chart). If you have completed those studies, then you know the whole gospel, who you are in Christ, and who your heavenly Father is. The four subsequent studies—*Your Foundation in Christ, Renewing Your Mind, Growing in Faith*, and *Your Life in Christ*—discussed issues related to your spiritual growth and what it means to live and minister to others in Christ (level two and three in the above chart).

This study, *Your Authority in Christ*, and the final study, *Your Ultimate Victory*, examine the enemies of our sanctification and how to overcome the world, the flesh, and the devil.

As you work through the six sessions in this Bible study, you will discover how Satan works in this world and how he attempts to oppose God, how good and evil spirits operate on the earth, how you can grasp your authority in Christ and overcome the enemy, what qualifications and limitations you have on spiritual authority, and how to protect yourself from Satan's attacks by putting on the armor of God. Keep in mind throughout this study that "you, dear children, are from God and have overcome [the enemy], because the one who is in you is greater than the one who is in the world" (1 John 4:4). Jesus has disarmed Satan, and the good angels outnumber the bad angels. Victory is assured for all those who put their faith in God.

Building your life on Christ requires the right foundation, which is your personal identity and security in Christ. For this reason, the Steps to Freedom in Christ will be mentioned during this study. This booklet can be purchased at any Christian bookstore or from Freedom in Christ Ministries. The Steps to Freedom in Christ is a repentance process that can help you resolve your personal and spiritual conflicts. The theology and application of the Steps is explained in the book *Discipleship Counseling*.

Before starting each daily reading, review the portion of Scripture listed for that day, then complete the questions at the end of each day's reading. These questions have been written to allow you to reflect on the material and apply to your life the ideas presented in the reading. At the end of each study, I have included a quote from a Church father illustrating the continuity of the Christian faith. Featured articles will appear in the text throughout the series, which are for the edification of the reader and not necessarily meant for discussion.

If you are part of a small group, be prepared to share your thoughts and insights with your group. You may also want to set up an accountability partnership with someone in your group to encourage you as you apply what you have learned in each session. For those of you who are leading a small group, there are leader tips at the end of this book that will help you guide your participants through the material.

As with any spiritual discipline, you will be tempted at times not to finish this study. There is a "sure reward" for those who make a "sure commitment." The VICTORY SERIES is far more than an intellectual exercise. The truth will not set you free if you only acknowledge it and discuss it on an intellectual level. For the truth to transform your life, you must believe it personally and allow it to sink deep into your heart. Trust the Holy Spirit to lead you into all truth, and enable you to be the person God has created you to be. Decide to live what you have chosen to believe.

Dr. Neil T. Anderson

The Origin of Evil

Missionaries who have been raised and educated in the United States are often confronted with the reality of the spiritual world in ways that they feel inadequate to deal with in foreign cultures. One such missionary was home on furlough and was suffering from the causalities of spiritual warfare. She was seeing her psychologist, psychiatrist, and her pastor once a week, just to hold her life together. The pastor was a former student of mine. He called me and said, "If you can't help her, we will have to commit her." The three of us met one Friday afternoon. Two and a half months later, I received the following letter:

> I've been wanting to write to you for awhile now, but I've waited this long to confirm to myself that this is truly "for reals" (as my four-year-old daughter says). I'd like to share an entry from my journal. I wrote this two days after our meeting.
>
> *"Since Friday afternoon I have felt like a different person. The fits of rage and anger are gone. My spirit is so calm and full of joy. I wake up singing to God in my heart. That edge of tension and irritation is gone. I feel so free. The Bible has been exciting and stimulating and more understandable*

than ever before. There was nothing "dramatic" that happened during the session on Friday, yet I know in the deepest part of my being that something has changed. I am no longer bound by accusations, doubt, and thoughts of suicide, murder, or other harm that come straight from hell to my head. There is a serenity in my mind and spirit and a clarity of consciousness that is profound.

"I've been set free! I'm excited and expectant about my future now. I know that I'll be growing spiritually again and will be developing in other ways as well. I look forward to discovering the person God has created and redeemed me to be, as well as the transformation of my marriage. It is so wonderful to have joy after so long a darkness."

It's been two and a half months since I wrote that entry, and I'm firmly convinced of the significant benefits of the Steps to Freedom in Christ. I've been in therapy for several months, and while I believe I was making some progress, there is no comparison with the steps I'm able to make now. My ability to process things has increased many fold. Not only is my spirit more serene but my head is also actually clearer! It's easier to make connections and integrate things now. It seems like everything is easier to understand now.

My relationship with God has changed significantly. For eight years I'd felt that He was distant from me. I was desperately crying out to Him to set me free—to release me from this bondage I was in. I wanted so badly to meet with Him again and know His presence was with me again. I needed to know Him as a friend and a companion, not as the distant authority figure He had become in my mind and experience. Since that day, I've seen my trust in Him grow, I've seen my ability to be honest with Him increase greatly. I really have been experiencing that spiritual growth I'd anticipated in my journal entry. It's great!

This testimony illustrates the comments of a well-known African bishop who was visiting the United States. After attending several Christian meetings associated with Mission America, he asked his host, Dr. Paul Cedar, "Why do you have so much counseling in America?" Dr. Cedar explained that there are, indeed, a lot of people who have a lot of problems. The bishop listened politely and responded, "Oh, I see. In America, you counsel people. In Africa, we repent."

Daily Readings

1. Satan	Ezekiel 28:1–19
2. The Fall of Lucifer	Isaiah 14:1–23
3. The Work of Satan	Job 1:6–12
4. The Names and Nature of Satan	Revelation 9:1–11
5. The Judgment and Defeat of Satan	John 12:23–33

1

Satan

Ezekiel 28:1–19

Key Point

Orthodox Christianity has always professed to believe in a personal devil.

Key Verse

In the pride of your heart you say, "I am a god."

Ezekiel 28:2

The word "Satan" is only mentioned three times in the Old Testament (see 1 Chronicles 21:1; Job 1:6–12; Zechariah 3:1–10). However, conservative scholars identify the serpent in Genesis 3 as Satan, or at least a beast that was possessed by Satan. Scripture says the serpent is "more crafty than any of the wild animals the LORD God had made" (Genesis 3:1). Satan's designations as "tempter" (Matthew 4:3) and the "ancient serpent" (Revelation 12:9) refer back to the Genesis passage.

Biblical scholars have noted that the characteristics about the king of Tyre in Ezekiel 28 do not seem applicable to a mere human being. The king sees himself as being as wise as a god (see verse 6) and wiser than Daniel (see verse 3). This proud person claims to be a god and sit on the throne of a god (see verse 2).

This is what the Lord had to say about him: "You were the seal of perfection, full of wisdom and perfect in beauty. You were in Eden, the garden of God. . . . You were anointed as a guardian cherub, for so I ordained you. You were on the holy mount of God; you walked among the fiery stones. You were blameless in your ways from the day you were created till wickedness was found in you. . . . So I drove you in disgrace from the mount of God, and I expelled you. . . . Your heart became proud on account of your beauty, and you corrupted your wisdom because of your splendor" (verses 12–17).

The Church has understood this passage to be speaking about the fall of the king of Tyre and the fall of Satan. Ezekiel is making a historical as well as a cosmic point about Satan as a created angelic being. At one time Satan had a privileged position with God, but he fell due to his own rebellious choice. The full character of Satan's evil nature is not fully developed in the Old Testament, but in the New Testament the term "Satan" occurs thirty-six times. Most references refer to him as a personal devil. That means the devil is a personality who is crafty and deceptive, as opposed to an impersonal force. Orthodox Christianity has always professed to believe in a personal devil.

Satan holds a position of great influence in the spiritual world. He has personal access to the presence of God, a privilege that will be taken away from him in the future. "The great dragon was hurled down—that ancient serpent called the devil, or Satan, who leads the whole world astray. He was hurled to the earth, and his angels with him" (Revelation 12:9). Satan is the ruler over a kingdom of evil that he executes with intelligent consistency. Because Satan is not omnipresent, he rules over the kingdom of darkness by delegating responsibility to "his angels" (see Matthew 25:41; Revelation 12:7).

Jesus said, "A time is coming and has now come when the true worshipers will worship the Father in the Spirit and in truth, for they are the kind of worshipers the Father seeks" (John 4:23). Our heavenly Father is seeking those who ascribe only to Him the divine attributes that only He possesses. They will know Christ from the Antichrist.

After the serpent deceived Eve, God said to the serpent, "Because you have done this, 'cursed are you above all the livestock and all the wild animals! You will crawl on your belly and you will eat dust all the days of your life'" (Genesis 3:14). What conclusions can you draw from that curse?

_____

_____

_____

What caused the fall of the "king of Tyre" and Satan?

_____

_____

_____

What point is Ezekiel making about Satan as a created angelic being?

_____

_____

_____

What difference does it make to you to know that Satan is a personality as opposed to an impersonal force?

_____

_____

_____

Why do you need to worship God in spirit and in truth?

_____

_____

_____

God made another being, in whom the disposition of the divine origin did not remain. Therefore, he was infected with his own envy, as with poison. So he passed from good to evil. Through his own will, which had been given to him by God unfettered, he acquired for himself a contrary name. From this, it appears that the source of all evils is envy. For he envied his predecessor [the Son], who through His steadfastness is acceptable and dear to God the Father. This person, who from good became evil by his own act, is called by the Greeks diabolos [slanderer]. We call him the Accuser, for he reports to God the faults to which he himself entices us.

Lactantius (AD 240–320)

2

The Fall of Lucifer

Isaiah 14:1–23

Key Point

Pride comes before a fall and rebellion is as the sin of divination.

Key Verses

As for you, you were dead in your transgressions and sins, in which you used to live when you followed the ways of this world and of the ruler of the kingdom of the air, the spirit who is now at work in those who are disobedient.

Ephesians 2:1–2

Isaiah 14:1–23 contains a prophecy against Sennacherib, who proclaimed himself king after conquering Babylon (see Isaiah 14:4). Although he is mighty now and able to inflict suffering and turmoil on his subjects (see verse 3), he shall be brought down to the grave and mocked (see verses 9–11). The passage refers to the king of Babylon, but the Church has also considered the verses that follow as a prophecy of the fall of Lucifer. Lucifer is Latin for "morning star" (verse 12). He is the symbolic representation of the king of Babylon in his pride, splendor, and fall. Satan is the head of this present world system and the invisible power behind the successive world rulers of Tyre, Babylon, Persia, Greece, and Rome.

This far-reaching passage goes beyond human history and marks the beginning of sin in the universe and the fall of Satan. The rule of Satan is not confined to his own person. All those who are dead in their trespasses and sins follow "the ways of this world and of the ruler of the kingdom of the air, the spirit who is now at work in those who are disobedient" (Ephesians 2:2). Satan operates his kingdom through a hierarchy of evil spirits and unregenerate people.

In the same way, the rule of God is not confined to His own Person. Jesus says, "Truly I tell you, whoever believes in me will do the works I have been doing, and they will do even greater things than these, because I am going to the Father" (John 14:12). As long as Jesus remained in the earth, His kingdom rule was confined to Himself. However, after being glorified, the Holy Spirit is now present in every believer. As believers, we will do greater things than Christ, because His presence is manifested all over the world in our lives. God rules His kingdom through ministering angels and through the lives of His children who are filled (controlled) by the Holy Spirit.

Lucifer was caught up with his own beauty and challenged the throne of God. He expressed his pride by saying five times "I will" (see Isaiah 14:13–14). But he was only a light bearer and not the source of light. As a created being, Lucifer could only reflect the glory of God. His pride and rebellion resulted in his expulsion from heaven. Now he is totally devoid of light. Satan is not some shady character who is naughty at times. He is the epitome of evil and the total absence of anything good.

In contrast, "God is light; in him there is no darkness at all" (1 John 1:5). At one time we were darkened in our understanding and separated from the life of God (see Ephesians 4:18). Then came Jesus, and "in him was life, and that life was the light of all mankind" (John 1:4). "For you were once darkness, but now you are light in the Lord. Live as children of light (for the fruit of the light consists in all goodness, righteousness and truth)" (Ephesians 5:8–9).

Do not look lightly on a "little" rebellion and a "little" pride. Saul did, and like Lucifer, he lost his privileged position. "For rebellion is like the sin of divination, and arrogance like the evil of idolatry. Because you have rejected the word of the LORD, he has rejected you as king" (1 Samuel 15:23).

What does the prophecy in Isaiah 14:1–23 reveal about Satan?

How does the "ruler of the kingdom of the air" rule in this world?

What led to Satan's downfall and expulsion from heaven? How should that serve as a warning to us?

How would you compare the sins of pride and rebellion to the more obvious sins of the flesh?

What do you think is at the heart of rebellion and pride?

_____

_____

_____

As a Jew Paul had been one of the "children of unbelief" in whom "the devil was at work," especially when he persecuted the church and the Christ of the Creator. On this account he says, "We were by nature children of wrath." But he says "by nature" so that a heretic could not argue that it was the Lord who created evil. We create the ground for the Savior's wrath ourselves.

Tertullian (AD 160–220)

3

The Work of Satan

Job 1:6–12

Key Point

Satan, the author of evil and the father of lies, relentlessly attacks the children of God, who is the author of life and the Spirit of truth.

Key Verse

The great dragon was hurled down—that ancient serpent called the devil, or Satan, who leads the whole world astray. He was hurled to the earth, and his angels with him.

Revelation 12:9

In the prologue to the book of Job, Satan appears with the angels who are gathering for their council meeting with the Lord. Satan came with the sons of God, but he is not one of them. God says to Satan, "'Have you considered my servant Job? There is no one on earth like him, he is blameless and upright, a man who fears God and shuns evil.' 'Does Job fear God for nothing?' Satan replied" (Job 1:8–9).

The question Satan asked is whether Job was serving God with a pure heart or for the fringe benefits of knowing Him. To find out, God allowed Satan to test Job by placing everything Job had in Satan's hands, though he could not take Job's life (see 1:12–22; 2:6–8). God has placed limits on what Satan can do. God is not the author of evil, but He will allow it within limits for our testing. Neither did God create Satan. God created Lucifer with a free will to serve Him. Satan is the result of Lucifer's choice to rebel against God.

Satan described his activity as "roaming throughout the earth, going back and forth in it" (1:7). He is engaged in a relentless global conflict against God and His people. He is the enemy of God and of truth (see Matthew 13:28, 39; 2 Thessalonians 2:9–12). He works through our weaknesses and limitations and employs the allurements of the world. He works in the realm of moral darkness (see Acts 26:18) as a tempter, enticing us to sin. His purpose is to get the children of God to live independently of their heavenly Father. When we sin, he acts as our accuser.

Jesus describes Satan's chief characteristic in John 8:44, which is also evident in the sons of the evil one: "You belong to your father, the devil, and you want to carry out your father's desires. He was a murderer from the beginning, not holding to the truth, for there is no truth in him. When he lies, he speaks his native language, for he is a liar and the father of lies."

Deception is Satan's primary strategy, and he has succeeded in leading the whole world astray (see Revelation 12:9). Satan masquerades as an angel of light, disguising his messengers of falsehood as messengers of truth (see 2 Corinthians 11:13–15). Those who give themselves over to evil become the agents of Satan. Jesus said to His disciples, "Have I not chosen you, the Twelve? Yet one of you is a devil!" (John 6:70). Paul said to the Jewish sorcerer, "You are a child of the devil and an enemy of everything that is right! You are full of all kinds of deceit and trickery" (Acts 13:10).

Satan is a counterfeiter. He sends false prophets and teachers. He sows counterfeit believers among the "people of the kingdom" (see Matthew 13:38). Satan leads people away by counterfeiting the true gifts of God. Apostate workers engage in religious activities without accepting the power of God's truth (see 2 Timothy 3:1–9). Satan blinds the minds of unbelievers "so that they cannot see the light of the gospel that displays the glory of Christ, who is the image of God" (2 Corinthians 4:4).

How would we know of Satan's activities if God hadn't revealed them in Scripture?

_____

_____

_____

If we didn't know that Satan is the father of lies and the instigator behind many clandestine acts, who would get the blame? How would we explain their actions?

_____

_____

_____

Does Satan work primarily overtly or covertly? Explain.

_____

_____

_____

Paul told the church in Corinth to hand a man who had been involved in incest "over to Satan for the destruction of the flesh, so that his spirit may be saved on the day of the Lord" (1 Corinthians 5:5). How is that similar and dissimilar to Job's experience? What application does that have for us today?

_____

_____

_____

Do you believe that God could use Satan to accomplish His will? Why or why not?

_____

_____

_____

When Paul says that this man must be delivered to Satan, he does not mean that he should be handed over to the power of the evil one. Rather, all the evils of this life, for example, diseases, sorrows, sufferings, and other circumstances, were attributed to Satan, and it is in this sense that Paul uses the term here. What he means is that this man should be exposed to the hardships of life.

Severian of Gabala (AD 380–425)

Paul says that the Corinthians [in 1 Corinthians 5:1–5] are to blame, because by taking pride in this man they have hindered him from repenting. Here he indicates that the problem is one for the whole church, not just the individual. This is why he uses the symbol of the leaven, which, although a small thing in itself, transforms the whole lump into its nature.

John Chrysostom (AD 347–407)

4

The Names and Nature of Satan

Revelation 9:1–11

Key Point

At the end of time every knee in heaven and on earth will bow to the name of Jesus.

Key Verses

Then war broke out in heaven. Michael and his angels fought against the dragon, and the dragon and his angels fought back. But he was not strong enough, and they lost their place in heaven. The great dragon was hurled down—that ancient serpent called the devil, or Satan, who leads the whole world astray.

Revelation 12:7–9

The term "satan" has the general meaning of "an adversary" or "an enemy." In 1 Samuel 29:4, "adversary" is used to describe David, who is considered an enemy in battle. In 1 Kings 11:14, 23, 25, it designates political adversaries of Solomon. In Psalm 109:6 (KJV), the word "satan" is used to refer to a human accuser.

When the definite article "the" is added, the term "the adversary" becomes a proper name and denotes the person of Satan. He is referred to as "the devil" thirty-three times, which means "the slanderer." The terms "Satan" and "devil" are essentially interchangeable. John called him "the angel of the Abyss, whose name in Hebrew is Abaddon, and in Greek is Apollyon" (Revelation 9:11). Both words mean "destruction" or "destroyer." The Abyss is the place of destruction. In the Bible, names are often more than labels for identification. In the case of Satan, they imply his character and purpose as well.

Satan is called "the accuser of our brothers and sisters, who accuses them before our God day and night" (Revelation 12:10). On the contrary, Jesus always lives to make intercession. He says "my grace is sufficient" (2 Corinthians 12:9), because He has died once for all our sins. Satan is called our "enemy" or "adversary" who "prowls around like a roaring lion looking for someone to devour" (1 Peter 5:8). In contrast, Jesus said, "You are my friends if you do what I command" (John 15:14). Paul also wrote, "What harmony is there between Christ and Belial" (2 Corinthians 6:15). *Belial* means worthlessness or wickedness.

The terms "the great dragon" and the "ancient serpent" (Revelation 12:9) are used figuratively of Satan to convey his craft and power and also the serpent's role as tempter in the Garden of Eden (see Genesis 3). He is "the evil one" (Matthew 13:38) who snatches away the good seed and sows the bad seed. Satan is "the father of lies" and "a murderer from the beginning" (John 8:44). He is "the ruler of the kingdom of the air" (Ephesians 2:2) who roams the earth and pollutes the atmosphere. Jesus called him "the prince of this world" (John 12:31; 14:30; 16:11); the ruling monarch in the kingdom of darkness who still dominates this world. Satan is "the tempter" (Matthew 4:3; 1 Thessalonians 3:5) who tried to entice Jesus to act independently of the Father.

When applied to character, the name says it all. "Everyone who calls on the name of the Lord will be saved" (Acts 2:21). "Salvation is found in no one else, for there is no other name under heaven given to mankind by which we must be saved" (Acts 4:12). "Therefore God exalted him to the highest place and gave him the name that is above every name, that at the name of Jesus every knee should bow, in heaven and on earth and under the earth, and every tongue acknowledge that Jesus Christ is Lord, to the glory of God the Father" (Philippians 2:9–11). You can rejoice if your name is written in the Lamb's Book of Life (see Revelation 3:5).

Why is every name associated with Satan a reference to his character or mission?

What can we know of Satan's work based on his name? How does that stand in stark contrast to the names applied to our Lord?

Why do we have to call on the name of the Lord to be saved?

Have you ever been labeled or called a derogatory name that impugned your character? If so, how did that make you feel?

Why is it important for you to understand the names and nature of Satan?

"As king they have over them the angel of the bottomless pit, whose name in Hebrew is 'Armageddon' [Abaddon], whose name in Greek is 'apollion,' and whose name in Latin is 'Exterminans'" [Revelation 9:11]. Although God is supremely good, by hidden yet just judgments He nevertheless allows an angel suitable for such persons to rule over them. For a person is awarded as servant to the one who conquered him. And so the apostle said that they had been handed over "to every wicked deception because they refused to love the truth and so to be saved. Therefore, God sends upon them a strong delusion that they might believe what is false and that all who did not believe the truth but consented to iniquity might be condemned" [2 Thessalonians 2:10–12]. The kind of work he did, therefore, was befitting to the character of his name, that is, the "exterminator."

Primasius of Hadrumetum (d. AD 560)

5

The Judgment and Defeat of Satan

John 12:23–33

Key Point

Satan's doom will be to share the eternal punishment of those whom he deceived.

Key Verse

And having disarmed the powers and authorities, he made a public spectacle of them, triumphing over them by the cross.

Colossians 2:15

The explicit purpose of Christ's coming into this world was to "destroy the devil's work" (1 John 3:8). We have the assurance that Satan will be driven out (see John 12:31). According to Jesus, he already stands condemned (see 16:11). The crucial battle between the kingdom of God and the kingdom of evil took place during the conflict between Christ and Satan. Satan's initial defeat came in the wilderness temptation at the beginning of our Lord's ministry (see Mark 1:12–13). Because Jesus did not succumb to the devil's temptations, during His ministry He was able to enter the strong man's house and plunder His goods (see Mark 3:27).

The decisive defeat of Satan occurred at the crucifixion and resurrection of Christ. At the cross, Christ judged Satan as a usurper and no longer the legitimate ruler of this world. The cross and the resurrection broke the power of Satan over humankind. The finished work of Christ resulted in three immediate benefits to us: we were made alive, we were forgiven, and the powers and authorities were disarmed (see Colossians 2:13–15).

At the cross, Jesus destroyed "him who holds the power of death—that is, the devil" (Hebrews 2:14). He continues to "free those who all their lives [have been] held in slavery by their fear of death" (verse 15). Jesus Christ has delivered those of us who have put our trust in Him from Satan's power.

Although judgment has already been pronounced on Satan, he is still permitted to operate as a usurper on earth until the time of his final imprisonment. As a dethroned monarch, he is allowed to rule those who accept his authority. Some have seen this truth foreshadowed by the anointing of David as the king of Israel, but Saul continued to rule over those who still acknowledged him as king. As followers of Jesus, we don't have to fear death or Satan. He no longer has authority over us and can do nothing to change our identity and position in Christ. When we put our faith in the saving work of our Lord Jesus Christ, we were delivered from the dominion of darkness and brought into the kingdom of God (see Colossians 1:12–13). We have to stand firm in our faith and rest in the finished work of Christ.

Jesus asserted that "the eternal fire" had been prepared for "the devil and his angels" (Matthew 25:41). Premillennialists believe the book of Revelation describes this final judgment of the devil. At the return of Christ, the devil will be confined to the bottomless pit for a thousand years, during which time the earth will be free from his deceptive and destructive influences (see Revelation 20:1–3). At the end of the thousand years, Satan will be loosed from his prison and will again deceive the inhabitants of the earth. Amillennialists believe this will all happen when Christ returns.

This final rebellion will be summarily crushed by divine action. According to John's vision, "the devil, who deceived them, was thrown into the lake of burning sulfur, where the beast and the false prophet had been thrown. They will be tormented day and night for ever and ever" (Revelation

20:10). Satan's destiny is to share the eternal punishment of those whom he deceived and refused to trust in Christ (see Revelation 20:12–14).

When was Satan's initial defeat? How was he defeated?

_____

_____

_____

What was the decisive defeat of Satan? What does that defeat mean for believers of Christ today?

_____

_____

_____

_____

What powers does Satan retain even though he is defeated? What does the Bible say will be his ultimate demise?

_____

_____

_____

_____

What power does Satan really have over you—or over any of God's children?

_____

_____

_____

If Satan knows his ultimate demise, why does he continue to strive against God and His Church?

He destroys the tyranny of the evil one who dominated us by deceit. By casting at him as a weapon the flesh that was vanquished in Adam, he overcame him. Thus what was previously captured for death conquers the conqueror and destroys his life by a natural death. It became poison to him in order that he might vomit up all those whom he had swallowed when held sway by having the power of death. But it became life to the human race by impelling the whole of nature to rise like dough to resurrection life. It was for this especially that the Logos, who is God, became human—something truly unheard of—and voluntarily accepted the death of the flesh.

Maximus the Confessor (AD 580–662)

Good and Evil Spirits

"A word was secretly brought to me, my ears caught a whisper of it. Amid disquieting dreams in the night, when deep sleep falls on people, fear and trembling seized me and made all my bones shake. A spirit glided past my face, and the hair on my body stood on end. It stopped, but I could not tell what it was. A form stood before my eyes, and I heard a hushed voice: 'Can a mortal be more righteous than God? Can even a strong man be more pure than his Maker?'"

Job 4:12–17

Some may be tempted to see this scene as a visitation from God, but was it? Does God speak secretly, or does He do everything in the light? "A spirit" is not "the Spirit." Saint Gregory the Great commented that Job's friends typifed teachers of false doctrines who pretended to hear hidden words from God in order to confuse the weak and to "cast a veil of reverence" over their preaching.

The experience mentioned above is presently happening all over the world. Ask people in any congregation if they have ever been awakened at night with an overwhelming sense of fear. It could have felt as if they were half asleep, and they could have felt a pressure on their chest or something grabbing their throat. When they tried to say something, they couldn't. You will find that a third or more of the people have had such an experience. This is a spiritual attack, and it can be resolved by submitting to God and resisting the devil, in that order (see James 4:7).

People with no discernment or biblical knowledge are unable to tell a bad spirit from an angel or the Holy Spirit. With the rise of New Age teaching, gullible people are actually aspiring to become channelers of spirits. They have no idea that they are mediums receiving information from demons, as the following testimony reveals:

> As a former channeler, let me share how psychics work. They only know what they are told by demons, and demons only know that which they have observed or what has been spoken out. For example, if my husband and I were talking about going to Hawaii for a vacation and I went to see a psychic, the person might say something like, "I see you on vacation somewhere warm. There is a beach and sand. You're with a tall dark man—your husband. I believe it is Hawaii." Of course, anyone would be impressed by that apparent knowledge of the unknown.
>
> I worked as a psychic and ran in circles with those who were "gifted" in this area. I got hooked at an early age. They were always able to tell me what had been spoken out and even some things that seemed might happen. For example, I have always been a writer (and musician), and they would tell me that I was talented and would succeed in both areas. However, everyone—even non-channelers—had told me that because they had seen my passion for writing. It was an obvious gift, and I was persistent. So, of course I would find ways to get published.
>
> Eventually that happened, but it did not happen in the time frame they had predicted. That was an unknown to them, so they bluffed their way through. Some of their future predictions happened, and some of them didn't. What I did notice was that a psychic could give intimate details about a person's past, but not his or her future. That was always vague and often untrue in the unfolding events.

The key to becoming a good psychic is submitting to "the spirit," which I was constantly told to do. I had the "gift," but it would be stronger or better if I'd only submit more. I was told that I was rebelling from my gift when I resisted.

God is gracious and merciful. There was always something (the Lord, no doubt) that held me back from fully committing. Even though I was not a believer in Christ, I eventually saw the inconsistency and deception and slowly stepped away. After becoming a believer and going through the Steps to Freedom in Christ, I was set free from my involvement in these areas and saw the entire deception clearly.

Daily Readings

1. Angels	Psalm 148:1–6
2. The Nature of Angels	Judges 13:2–21
3. The Ministry of Angels	Acts 12:6–11
4. The Nature of Demons	Luke 11:14–26
5. The Work of Demons	Revelation 12:9–12

1

Angels

Psalm 148:1–6

Key Point

Angels are spiritual beings who in the Bible appeared to good people as men.

Key Verse

Do not forget to show hospitality to strangers, for by so doing some people have shown hospitality to angels without knowing it.

Hebrews 13:2

The word "angel" means "messenger." The term primarily refers to heavenly beings, though it can mean a human messenger such as a prophet (see Haggai 1:13) or a priest (see Malachi 2:7). The Bible also refers to these angelic beings as "sons of God" (Genesis 6:2–4; Job 1:6 KJV); "heavenly beings" (Psalm 29:1); "holy ones" (Psalm 89:5); "heavenly host" (Luke 2:13); and "hosts," as in the phrase "LORD of hosts" (1 Samuel 1:11 KJV). The seraphim in Isaiah 6 also belong to the order of angels.

Angels are spiritual and majestic in nature. They existed before the creation of Adam and Eve, and their purpose is to execute God's will (see Psalm 148:2–5). They can pass from the spiritual realm to the physical realm at will, unimpeded by natural boundaries (see Acts 12:7). Angels also have superior intellect and wisdom (see 2 Samuel 14:17, 20), but they are not omniscient (see Matthew 24:36). According to Jesus, they do not marry and they will live forever (see Luke 20:35–36). Psalm 103:20 is a good summary of the role and nature of angels: "Praise the LORD, you his angels, you mighty ones who do his bidding, who obey his word."

In the Bible, good angels consistently appear to people in human form on earth. They never appear as animals, reptiles, birds, or material objects. There is no biblical record showing that a good angel ever appeared to wicked people or warned them of any danger. They are "ministering spirits sent to serve those who will inherit salvation" (Hebrews 1:14). Good angels always appeared to good people in human form as men. They never appeared as women or children, and they were always clothed. Just as Christ appeared in human form, so angels identified with humans in form, in speech, and in deed.

Sometimes the angels in the Bible were disguised so well as men that the people did not at first recognize them as angels. Abraham entertained "three men" as dinner guests. One remained to talk while the other two left to spend the night with Lot, who thought they were men (see Genesis 18:2; 19:1). Joshua did not know that the man standing before him was God's angel (see Joshua 5:13). Neither did Gideon realize that his guest was an angel until the angel made an offering of his meal (see Judges 6:21–22).

Occasionally, angels displayed themselves with a heavenly countenance and clothing that revealed the glory of God. In Luke 24:4, while the two women were lingering at the empty tomb of Jesus, "suddenly two men in clothes that gleamed like lightning stood beside them." In Daniel 10:5–6, the prophet gave a colorful description of an angel. On numerous occasions, angels were also described as "a man," or at least of having the appearance of a man (Ezekiel 40:3; Daniel 10:18; Zechariah 2:1).

Peter warns the Church about false teachers "who follow the corrupt desire of the flesh and despise authority. Bold and arrogant, they are not afraid to heap abuse on celestial beings; yet even angels, although they are stronger and more powerful, do not heap abuse on such beings when bringing judgment on them from the Lord" (2 Peter 2:10–11). Such restraint only reveals the angels' godly character, which stands in stark contrast to evil spirits.

What are some of the attributes of angels?

_____

_____

In what ways do angels appear to people in the Bible?

_____

_____

How can angels be distinguished from evil men and evil spirits?

_____

_____

Why do you think God uses angels in the appearance of men to enact His purposes?

_____

_____

_____

Have you ever thought you might have encountered an angel? How would you know if you had?

_____

_____

_____

The angels who dwell in holiness are stronger than human beings, even if it is true that we are more blessed than they are. Angels look after holy people who are helped by them, since human beings cannot offer consolation to angels.

Didymus the Blind (AD 313–398)

2

The Nature of Angels

Judges 13:2–21

Key Point

Angels are sent by God to fulfill a specific mission.

Key Verse

The angel of the Lord encamps around those who fear him, and he delivers them.

Psalm 34:7

In the original creation, all angels were good. However, when Satan led a rebellion against God, he took a third of the angels with him (see Revelation 12:7–9). Now God commands His good angels and Satan commands a horde of bad angels, who are identified as evil spirits or demons.

Contrary to the good angels, demons never appear in human form. People do see demonic apparitions, or ghost-like appearances, but it is not "flesh and blood" (Ephesians 6:12). They are spirits who serve the evil desires of Satan. Satan functions as the ruler of this world through a demonic hierarchy. He is not omnipresent, so he reigns over his kingdom of darkness through rulers, authorities, powers of this dark world and "the spiritual forces of evil in the heavenly realms" (Ephesians 6:12).

In contrast to the evil nature of demons, good angels are called "the holy angels" (Luke 9:26), "the angels of God" (Luke 12:8) and "God's angels" (Hebrews 1:6). Jesus spoke of "his angels" (Matthew 16:27) and "angels in heaven" (Matthew 22:30). Paul referred to God's "powerful angels" (2 Thessalonians 1:7).

Of these good angels, only two in the Bible are mentioned by name. The first is Michael, whom Jude calls the archangel (see Jude 1:9). Michael disputed with Satan concerning the body of Moses and invoked the name of the Lord to rebuke him. In Daniel, Michael is called "one of the chief princes" (10:13). In Revelation, Michael is portrayed as the commander of the army of good angels who defeated and expelled the bad angels from heaven (12:7–8).

Gabriel is the other angel named in the Bible. He is the chief messenger angel who announced the births of John the Baptist and Jesus (see Luke 1:11–13, 19, 26–38). He interpreted Daniel's dream and delivered God's decree during the same mission (see Daniel 8:15–27).

"The angel of the Lord" seems to be a unique angel in the Old Testament. This angel announced the birth of Samson (see Judges 13:3–5) much like Gabriel did to Mary. When Manoah asked the angel of the Lord what his name was, he replied, "Why do you ask my name? It is beyond understanding" (verse 18). The use of the definite article "the" in "the angel of the Lord" has led some to speculate that this may be a preincarnate appearance of Christ. The same speculation has been made about the "man" who wrestled with Jacob and told him that he had struggled with God (see Genesis 32:22–31).

Several conclusions can be drawn from the angelic visitation to Manoah. First, angels have a specific assignment from God, which they strictly follow. Manoah prayed that God would send the angel again to teach them how to raise the child, and the Lord granted a second visit, but the angel simply repeated his earlier message. Second, they communicate audibly in the same language and through the same medium that humans do. Third, they take on a physical form that can be seen by any person present. Fourth, they may not always be recognized as angelic beings, but they are recognized as men of God (see Judges 13:6, 16). Fifth, they can change their form as they depart from our presence (see verse 20). All this stands in stark contrast to demons.

What are some of the definitive differences between angels and demons?

What roles did Michael and Gabriel play?

Who is "the angel of the Lord" in the Old Testament?

Have you ever considered the fact that you may have a guardian angel? If so, what difference does that make to you?

What is the practical significance of learning about "celestial beings"?

Let us consider the whole multitude of His angels—how they stand ready to minister to His will. For the Scripture says, "Ten thousand times ten thousand stood around Him, and thousands of thousands ministered to Him."

Clement of Rome (d. AD 101)

3

The Ministry of Angels

Acts 12:6–11

Key Point

Angels execute God's will in heaven and on earth.

Key Verse

Are not all angels ministering spirits sent to serve those who will inherit salvation?

Hebrews 1:14

Angels are mediators of God's love and goodwill toward humankind, and their mission is always benevolent, which can be summarized in the following five ways.

First, *angels announce and forewarn.* An angel announced in advance to Abraham and Sarah the conception and birth of their son Isaac (see Genesis 18:9–14). The angel of the Lord foretold the birth of Samson (see Judges 13:2–24). Gabriel announced the birth of John the Baptist and Jesus (see Luke 1:13, 30). An angel announced the birth of Jesus to the shepherds, and suddenly a chorus of heavenly hosts joined them in praising God. Angels also forewarned the righteous of imminent danger. An angel forewarned Abraham and Lot about the destruction of Sodom and Gomorrah (see Genesis 18:16–19:29). An angel also warned Joseph to flee to Egypt (see Matthew 2:13).

Second, *angels guide and instruct*. Abraham had repeated conversations with angels, and they guided him during his sojourn (see Genesis 24:7). When Moses led the Israelites out of Egypt, the angel of God guided them (see Exodus 14:19). During the Exodus, God told them, "See, I am sending an angel ahead of you to guard you along the way and to bring you to the place I have prepared" (23:20). An angel gave instructions to Cornelius (see Acts 10:3–7).

Third, *angels guard and defend*. "The angel of the LORD encamps around those who take refuge in him" (Psalm 34:7). An angel made Balaam revise his prophecy and rewrite his sermon (see Numbers 22:21–38). God's angelic army stood by to defend Elisha and his servant (see 2 Kings 6:17). An angel prevented Abraham from sacrificing Isaac (see Genesis 22:9–12) and protected the lives of Daniel and his three Hebrew friends (see Daniel 3:28; 6:22). The angel of death slew the firstborn of Egypt to force Pharaoh to release the Israelites (see Exodus 12:23). The angel of the Lord slew the army of Sennacherib to keep him from destroying Jerusalem (see 2 Kings 19:35). Jesus said He could have called on twelve legions of angels to save Himself (see Matthew 26:53).

John Patton, a missionary in the New Hebrides, was once surrounded by hostile natives who were intent on burning down his mission headquarters. He and his wife were alone. They prayed for divine protection all night and were amazed the next morning to see the attackers leave for no apparent reason. A year later, the chief of the tribe converted to Christ, and John asked why he and his men had left that night. The chief replied in surprise, "Who were all those men you had there with you—hundreds of men in shining garments?"[1]

Fourth, *angels minister to our needs*. Peter was in great need when an angel released his chains and marched him out of prison. An angel ministered to Elijah when he was exhausted and fed him some hot cakes and water (see 1 Kings 19:5–7). After Jesus fasted for forty days and was tempted by the devil, the "angels attended him" (Mark 1:13).

Fifth, *angels assist in judgment.* When the people shouted that Herod spoke as God, "Immediately, because Herod did not give praise to God, an angel of the Lord struck him down, and he was eaten by worms and died" (Acts 12:23). The sheep and the goats will be divided "when the Son of Man comes in his glory, and all the angels with him" (Matthew 25:31).

How in the Bible did angels announce God's messages and forewarn people?

_____

_____

_____

How did angels guide and instruct people?

_____

_____

_____

How did angels guard and defend people? Is that still happening today?

_____

_____

_____

Why do you think we are not more aware of the good work angels are doing today?

_____

_____

_____

Does it comfort you to know that ministering angels are active in the kingdom of God at this present time? Why or why not?

_____

_____

_____

Why was this not done through themselves [escaping from prison]? In this way God honors them [Peter and Paul], rescuing them through angels. Why did it not happen like this in the case of Paul [compare Acts 12:6–11 with Acts 16:25–33]? With good reason, because the prison guard was to be converted, while here only the apostle was to be released. In different ways God disposes different things. There, it is well for Paul to sing hymns; here, for Peter to sleep.

John Chrysostom (AD 347–407)

4

The Nature of Demons

Luke 11:14–26

Key Point

Demons are not benign spirit guides; they are evil messengers of Satan.

Key Verse

The next day an evil spirit from God came forcefully on Saul.

1 Samuel 18:10

After Jesus cast out a demon that had rendered a man mute, His detractors accused Him of casting out demons by the power of "Beelzebul, the prince of demons" (Luke 11:15). Jesus' following discussion about demons in verses 16–26 reveals a great deal about their nature and personality.

First, *demons can exist inside or outside of humans.* Demons have no physical means of expressing themselves except through human or animal agents. They seem to find a measure of rest in organic beings, even preferring swine to nothingness (see Mark 5:12). Evil spirits may assert territorial rights and be associated with certain geographical locations.

Second, *demons are able to travel at will.* Being spiritual entities, demons are not subject to the physical barriers of the natural world. The walls of church buildings do not provide a sanctuary, nor does our skin serve as a spiritual barrier. This is why we put on the armor of God. The only true sanctuary is our position in Christ.

Third, *demons are able to communicate with each other.* They can speak to humans through a human subject, as when they spoke to Christ through the Gadarene demoniac (see Matthew 8:28–34). We can also pay attention to deceiving spirits in our minds, which Paul warned us about: "But I am afraid that just as Eve was deceived by the serpent's cunning, your minds may somehow be led astray from your sincere and pure devotion to Christ" (2 Corinthians 11:3). People all over the world are struggling with condemning and blasphemous thoughts that are not of their choosing.

Fourth, *every evil spirit has a separate identity.* "When an impure spirit comes out of a person, it goes through arid places seeking rest and does not find it. Then it says, 'I will return to the house I left'" (Luke 11:24). Notice the use of personal pronouns. Demons are thinking personalities, not impersonal forces. Demons are like cockroaches. They operate under the cloak of darkness, and when the light is turned on, they scurry for the shadows. Their mission is always clandestine, and even their victims are not aware that they are being deceived.

Fifth, *demons have the ability to remember and make plans.* They can leave a person, remember the former state of the person, and come back with other demons. They obviously have the ability to think strategically.

Sixth, *demons are able to evaluate and make decisions.* The demons found "the house swept clean and put in order" (Luke 11:25). They can evaluate the condition of an intended victim and take advantage of a person's vulnerability.

Seventh, *demons are able to combine forces.* Notice in verse 26 that the one spirit joined with a group of seven other spirits, making the state of the victim worse than before. In the case of the Gadarene demoniac, a number of them had united together—hence their name "Legion" (Mark 5:9).

Eighth, *demons vary in degrees of wickedness.* The first demon brought back seven others "more wicked than itself" (Luke 11:26). Jesus indicated degrees of wickedness and power when he said, "This kind can come out only by prayer" (Mark 9:29). These variations in power and wickedness fit the hierarchy described in Ephesians 6:12.

Why do demons look for animate subjects to inhabit?

Why are natural barriers of no use in spiritual warfare?

Why do we need to take every thought captive to the obedience of Christ?

Is Paul's concern that our minds could be led astray, your concern as well? Why or why not?

If Satan is disarmed, why do you need to be alert and stand firm in your faith?

Furthermore, we are instructed by our sacred books how from certain angels, who fell of their own free will, there sprang a more wicked demon brood, condemned of God. . . . Their great business is the ruin of mankind. So, from the start, spiritual wickedness sought our destruction. Accordingly, they inflict upon our bodies diseases and other grievous calamities. And by violent assaults, they hurry the soul into sudden and extraordinary excesses. . . . By an influence equally obscure, demons . . . breathe into the soul, and rouse up its corruptions with furious passions and vile excesses.

Tertullian (AD 160–220)

5

The Work of Demons

Revelation 12:9–12

Key Point

The major work of demons is to tempt, accuse, and deceive the minds of people.

Key Verse

We know that anyone born of God does not continue to sin; the One who was born of God keeps them safe, and the evil one cannot harm them.

1 John 5:18

The Bible records extreme cases in which demons actually inhabited humans. In Mark 1:21–28, a demon spoke through a man in a synagogue. "'Be quiet!' said Jesus sternly. 'Come out of him!' The impure spirit shook the man violently and came out of him with a shriek" (verses 25–26). The Gadarene demoniac had many demons in him (see Mark 5:1–20). He exhibited supernatural strength by breaking the chains that bound him, and no human was strong enough to subdue him. Somehow these demons were able to control the man's central nervous system, enabling them to speak through the man. When the evil spirits left, the man's rational capacities were restored.

Another man brought his son to Jesus saying, "A spirit seizes him and he suddenly screams; it throws him into convulsions so that he foams at the mouth. It scarcely ever leaves him and is destroying him" (Luke 9:39). This was not a natural epileptic seizure. Jesus rebuked the evil spirit, healed the boy, and gave him back to his father (see verse 42).

Likewise, a woman in a synagogue "had been crippled by a spirit for eighteen years. She was bent over and could not straighten up at all" (Luke 13:11). This was not osteoporosis. Jesus said Satan had kept her bound (see verse 16). More than 25 percent of those physically healed in the Gospel of Mark are the result of their having been set free from demonic influences. Most physical illnesses come on us naturally, such as epilepsy and osteoporosis, but there may be another cause. We would have nothing to lose—but maybe much to gain—by verbally saying, "Lord, I submit my body to You as a living sacrifice, and I ask You to fill me with Your Holy Spirit. In the name and authority of the Lord Jesus Christ, I command Satan and all evil spirits to leave my presence."

The major spiritual work of demons is to tempt, accuse, and deceive the minds of people. It is not uncommon for the secular world to diagnose certain individuals as being mentally ill when the real issue is the spiritual battle being waged for their minds. "The Spirit clearly says that in later times some will abandon the faith and follow deceiving spirits and things taught by demons" (1 Timothy 4:1). If we are deceived and believe a lie, it affects our mental and emotional health, which often shows up physically as a psychosomatic illness.

Every psychiatrist, counselor, and social worker tries to help their clients deal with "voices" in their heads. They will likely explain that the cause is a chemical imbalance and justify their conclusions by saying, "I gave them an antipsychotic medication, and the voices stopped." All they did was narcotize the person. Take away the medicine and the voices are back, so nothing was cured. Many people drink and take drugs because they have no mental peace.

Of course there are neurological problems, but you also need to ask yourself some serious questions: Can a chemical imbalance create a personality and a thought? Can neurotransmitters randomly create a thought that I am opposed to thinking? Did I make a conscious choice to think that thought? Did I want to think that thought? If the answers are no, you may want to consider submitting to God and resisting the devil (see James 4:7) before seeing your secular doctor.

What was the mental state of the Gadarene demoniac when he was set free? What does that tell us?

How can we know the difference between a neurological problem and a spiritual battle for the mind?

Why does Paul urge us by the mercies of God to submit our bodies to God as a living sacrifice, to put on the armor of God, and to take every thought captive to the obedience of Christ?

How can we know the difference between a neurological problem and a spiritual battle for the mind?

Have you ever been plagued by condemning and blasphemous thoughts? If so, how can you tell whether those are your own thoughts or are from the enemy?

You can evaluate your spiritual condition by being alone and seeing how well you tolerate silence. Is there a peace of God guarding your heart and your mind, or are you mentally distracted? Do you have complete control of your mind? Why or why not?

_____

_____

_____

_____

The devil, however, as he is the apostate angel, can only go to this length, as he did at the beginning, to deceive and lead astray the mind of man into disobeying the commandments of God, and gradually to darken the hearts.

Irenaeus (AD 130–202)

Mental Illness?

Millions of people struggle with their mental health, and most suffer in silence. Nobody wants to reveal what is going on in his or her mind. Some actually fear the prospect of insanity. I received the following testimony from such a lady who attended a Discipleship Counseling conference.

It is by God's grace that I attended the conference. I had no idea what would be discussed, but God knew and arranged for me to be there. Thank You, Jesus. It was not easy getting there, as the voices in my head made me walk out halfway through the first night and halfway out of the parking lot before the second night even started. Now I know why.

At the conference my worst nightmares were laid to rest and I learned the truth about the voices I was hearing in my mind. It was the first time in my life someone attempted to explain an aspect of "mental illness" without me having to cringe and throw up. It would have been embarrassing, as I was sitting on the front row!

This is truly one of the happiest days of my life. What a relief to know that I am sane. For thirty years I begged God to save me from the pits of hell—from "mental illness." I have lived in fear all my life that I would be crazy like the rest of my family. I worried that I was only fooling myself that I was sane, because I had been "covering up" by serving God all these years. I was so terrified to tell anyone about the voices that I chose suicide instead. My marriage was being destroyed by those voices, and I knew that if I told my husband, he would have me locked up and put in a one-size-fits-all white jacket for the rest of my life. What is even scarier is that my in-laws would have beat him to it! I saw no way out.

I shuddered at the thought of living like my mother for the rest of my life. She is the victim of a split personality. As a child, I didn't know which person she was going to be from one minute to the next. It was a horrible childhood, and she actually tried to kill me three times that I can vividly remember before the age of four. She sexually abused all of her five children. I was the only one she continued with well into my teens. She threatened to kill me all the time, and I knew she had already attempted it, so I lived in tremendous fear all my life.

My mother told all of us from the time we were born that we were born to a crazy family and needed psychiatrists. If you can believe it, she was the head of the Bible school based from our church, and my father traveled as an evangelist with our denomination for more than thirty years! Naturally, my view of God hasn't been too clear. I am the only member of my family who hasn't suffered a nervous breakdown. I simply refused to do so. Now I know I never will.

I know that I am okay and not crazy. It is a relief that others besides me hear those same voices. I am not alone, and I don't have to be afraid anymore. I can be free. You can't imagine what it feels like to get out of this prison.

My first recollection of the voices (which were actually more like screaming) is that they always woke me up at exactly 3:15 a.m. For years and years I have been terrified of seeing 3:15 a.m. on the digital clock, and I stopped looking at the clock when the voices came. Tonight I woke up at exactly 3:15 a.m. and immediately checked the clock. This time there were no voices, and I started crying. I knew it was God. I didn't have to be afraid anymore. It is finally over!

I have asked Christians all over the world if they have ever been awakened (like this woman) at a precise time in the night, like 3:00 a.m., and I have never seen less than one-third of the hands raised. Among the leadership of more high-profile ministries, the percentage is higher. I have had many Christian leaders say they have been awakened at 3:00 a.m. and have wondered why that is the case. In the testimony above, I have no idea why the woman was awakened at 3:15 a.m.—it seems to be an anomaly. People naturally wake up at night for many reasons, but when they wake up at a specific time on a number of occasions, it suggests that something else is at play.

I have had the privilege of helping several people overcome satanic ritual abuse, and they have all said that 3:00 a.m. is prime time in the demonic world. I can't prove that, nor do I need to do so. If it is a spiritual attack, just remember that greater is He who is in you than he who is in the world (see 1 John 4:4). It is no sin to be under attack. Just submit to God, resist the devil, and go back to sleep. Take no pride for not experiencing any spiritual opposition to what you are doing, or not doing.

Overcoming the Opposition

"It is not the critic who counts; not the man who points out how the strong man stumbles, or where the doer of deeds could have done them better. The credit belongs to the man who is actually in the arena, whose face is marred by dust and sweat and blood; who strives valiantly; who errs, who comes short again and again, because there is no effort without error and shortcoming; but who does actually strive to do the deeds; who knows great enthusiasms, the great devotions; who spends himself in a worthy cause; who at the best knows in the end the triumph of high achievement, and who at the worst, if he fails, at least fails while daring greatly, so that his place shall never be with those cold and timid souls who neither know victory nor defeat."[1]

—Theodore Roosevelt

Daily Readings

1. The Enemies of Our Sanctification	Jeremiah 17:1–18
2. Defining the Flesh	2 John 1:1–13
3. Overcoming the Old Nature	Romans 8:1–39
4. Defining the World	Zephaniah 1:14–18; 2:1–15
5. Overcoming the World	Nahum 1:1–15

1

The Enemies of Our Sanctification

Jeremiah 17:1–18

Key Point

If you aren't encountering any opposition, you aren't growing.

Key Verse

I have fought the good fight, I have finished the race, I have kept the faith.

2 Timothy 4:7

Jeremiah paints a bleak picture for those who trust in themselves and depend on their own strength and resources (see Jeremiah 17:5). Before Christ, our hearts were deceitful and beyond human cure (see verse 9). But if we trust in the Lord, who searches our hearts, then we shall "be like a tree planted by the water" (verse 8). The consistent message in Scripture is that we must depend on the Lord for salvation and for sanctification (see verse 14).

63

Children of God are like diamonds in the rough. They begin their Christian walk looking like a lump of coal. They may look pretty bad and be messy to work with, but given enough time and pressure, every lump of coal has the potential to become a brilliant diamond. If you remove coal from the pressures of the earth and introduce impurities into its chemical composition, it will never reach its potential. Staying pure and remaining under pressure is what makes a diamond out of coal.

Unlike a lump of coal, we have a part to play in the sanctifying process. We cannot just "let go and let God" be the One who perfects us. We should rest in the finished work of Christ, abide in Christ, and live by faith in the power of the Holy Spirit. However, we don't have a passive role in the sanctifying process. We have to assume our responsibility to overcome the world, the flesh, and the devil. Therefore, we "continue to work out [our] salvation with fear and trembling, for it is God who works in [us] to will and to act in order to fulfill his good purpose" (Philippians 2:12–13).

We don't work *for* our salvation—we work it out. Paul describes this working out as a struggle, or, literally, a wrestling (see Ephesians 6:12 KJV). The Greek word implies a hand-to-hand fight, and Paul admonishes us to "fight the battle well" (1 Timothy 1:18). "But you, man of God, flee from all this, and pursue righteousness, godliness, faith, love, endurance and gentleness. Fight the good fight of the faith" (6:11–12). Our ultimate victory is certain, but that doesn't eliminate the present battle, which often intensifies when we start bearing fruit. The power of sin is most evident when we seriously challenge it. Temptation is no struggle if we continuously give in to it.

A professional counselor once said that he had never encountered any demonic spirits in fifteen years of counseling. After attending a Discipleship Counseling conference, he said, "I soon discovered that every one of my clients was being deceived, and so was I." Why didn't the counselor see it before? For the same reason many pastors and Bible teachers don't see it. We will not encounter much opposition if all we are doing is listening, explaining, and offering advice. The opposition comes only when we seek to resolve personal and spiritual conflicts through genuine repentance and faith in God.

A well-known Christian psychiatrist was asked, "What is your cure rate? He said, "I don't cure anyone; I help them cope." Some say, "God cures the soul; we only care for it." It is good to acknowledge our limitations, but if God wants to cure the soul and has chosen to work through godly people within the Church to accomplish that, why are we lowering the bar?

Why is it such a struggle to overcome the world, the flesh, and the devil?

Why is there a lot more "coal" than "diamonds"?

In what ways have we lowered the bar? In other words, why do we seek to offer information but not transformation?

How much are you helped if someone is able to accurately explain why you are messed up? Does that by itself resolve your problem? For instance, if you could explain why someone is drinking too much, would that help him stop drinking?

Is it worth the struggle to overcome the world, the flesh, and the devil? What is to be gained if you do and lost if you don't?

And when he says "with fear and trembling" [Philippians 2:12] see how he assuages the pain of it. For what does he say? "It is God who works in you." "Do not be afraid," he says, "because I said 'with fear and trembling.' I did not say it to make you give up, thinking virtue impossible of attainment, but so that you may carry on, so that you may not collapse.". . . He says not "I run" but "I press on" [Philippians 3:12]. Consider how the pursuer strains in his pursuit. He sees nothing, he thrusts away all who impede him with great force, he cherishes his mind, his eye, his strength, his soul and his body, looking at nothing other than the crown.

John Chrysostom (AD 347–407)

2

Defining the Flesh

2 John 1:1–13

Key Point

We have the choice of living according to the flesh or living according to the Spirit.

Key Verse

So I say, walk by the Spirit, and you will not gratify the desires of the flesh.

Galatians 5:16

One of the most dangerous heresies that confronted the Early Church in the second century was Gnosticism. The Gnostics taught that the spirit is good and that matter is evil. Therefore, our natural bodies are evil, but God is good because He is a Spirit. Salvation comes by special knowledge (*gnosis* is Greek for "knowledge") that enables us to escape from the body. The Gnostics denied the fact that Christ came in the flesh. Anyone who did not acknowledge Jesus as coming in the flesh was a deceiver (see 1 John 4:1–3; 2 John 1:7).

Some people influenced by Gnosticism taught that Jesus only *seemed* to have a body—a heretical view called Docetism. Others held that the "divine Jesus" joined the "man Jesus" at His baptism and left before the "man Jesus" died—a heresy called Cerinthianism. Because the body was evil, it was to be treated harshly.

The term "flesh" has many meanings in Scripture. In some instances it refers to the physical body. At times it refers to the whole person. John said of Jesus, "The Word became flesh and made his dwelling among us" (John 1:14). In such uses there is no concept of sinfulness or evil. Jesus never sinned, and His body was never evil.

The common thread for all the uses of the word "flesh" is the idea of weakness or a transitory nature. Compared to the spirit, which denotes life and power, the flesh is weak. It is this concept of weakness that has contributed to the use of the term "flesh" for that which is sinful or contrary to God. Humans, as flesh, are not only frail as creatures but also frail morally. Apart from God, humans are no match for the power of sin and consequently come under its bondage.

The use of the word "flesh" in reference to humankind's propensity to sin is prominent in the New Testament. It may be defined as existence apart from God. It represents our "old nature" before coming to Christ when we were "in Adam" or "in the flesh." Paul wrote, "Those who are in the flesh cannot please God. However, you are not *in the flesh* but *in the Spirit*, if indeed the Spirit of God dwells in you. But if anyone does not have the Spirit of Christ, he does not belong to Him" (Romans 8:8–9 NASB, emphasis added). In that one verse, Paul described the Trinity, interchanging "Spirit of God" with "Spirit of Christ." Because all believers are "in Christ," they are also "in the Spirit."

In Galatians 5:17, Paul wrote, "For the flesh sets its desire against the Spirit, and the Spirit against the flesh; for these are in opposition to one another" (NASB). They are in opposition because the Holy Spirit and God the Father are one. The flesh is self-centered and functions independently of God. The flesh seeks life on human terms and standards rather than on God's.

Our bodies are not sinful, but our minds retain certain flesh patterns that we learned before we came to Christ. In addition, we still have certain physical cravings that we have to subdue. Satan will work through those mental flesh patterns and cravings enticing us to live independently of God.

What was Gnosticism? How did it represent a problem for the Early Church?

_____

_____

_____

What does the term "flesh" mean in Scripture?

_____

_____

_____

How can you know whether you are living according to the flesh or living according to the Spirit?

_____

_____

_____

Why do you still have the propensity to sin? Do you believe you have the power to say no to sin? Why or why not?

_____

_____

_____

How can you manage self-control if it is a fruit of the Spirit?

_____

_____

_____

For a person to change and become good and subject to God is easy. . . . If we give our souls up to the Spirit and persuade our flesh to recognize its proper position, we shall make our souls spiritual as well. But if we are lazy we shall make our souls carnal. For since it was not natural necessity which put the gift into us but freedom of choice, it now rests with us which way we shall choose to go.

John Chrysostom (AD 347–407)

3

Overcoming the Old Nature

Romans 8:1–39

Key Point

It is our responsibility to crucify the flesh and all its sinful passions.

Key Verse

Those who live according to the flesh have their minds set on what the flesh desires; but those who live in accordance with the Spirit have their minds set on what the Spirit desires.

Romans 8:5

Before Christ, our total person was dominated by the flesh and oriented toward sin. Now that Christ dwells within us, our hearts are oriented toward God, but we still have a remnant of propensity toward self-autonomy (flesh or old nature). We can overcome this by the power of the Spirit. The old *I* died with Christ and has risen to a new *I* with a new heart and a new orientation.

Notice this shift from old *I* to the new *I* in Galatians 2:20: "I have been crucified with Christ and I no longer live, but Christ lives in me. The life I

71

now live in the body, I live by faith in the Son of God." This new orientation toward God radiates outwardly to increasingly minimize the propensity of the old nature. The Holy Spirit dwells in the new heart and seeks to fill (control) the entire person.

At salvation, the old self was crucified (see Romans 6:6). The finished work of Christ made that possible when we received Him by faith. Paul says to the new believer, "Those who belong to Christ Jesus have crucified the flesh with its passions and desires" (Galatians 5:24). The old self was crucified with Christ, but it is our responsibility to crucify the old nature and to put the old nature (flesh) to death. In repentance we crucified everything we knew to be wrong. We took our old self-centered nature with all its passions and desires and nailed it to the cross.

The reality of our actions is experienced only in accord with the faith in which it is done. We crucified everything we knew to be wrong with all the faith we had at that time. However, our knowledge of the truth and our response in faith were not yet mature and complete. We grow as we appropriate more and more of Christ's life by the power of the Holy Spirit. As we grow, the reality of what we did in principle (that is, crucifying the flesh and its old self-centered influence) becomes increasingly more real in our experience. As long as we choose to believe the truth and live by faith in the power of the Holy Spirit, the flesh will be rendered inoperative.

Crucifying the flesh is a mental battle. "Those who live according to the flesh have their minds set on what the flesh desires; but those who live in accordance with the Spirit have their minds set on what the Spirit desires" (Romans 8:5). The channels of temptation to live independently of God are the lust of the flesh, the lust of the eyes, and the boastful pride of life. If we set our minds on those objects, we are living according to the flesh, and the deeds of the flesh will become evident (see Galatians 5:19). If we set our minds on the things above, we are living by the Spirit (see Colossians 3:2).

Crucifying the flesh is also a crisis of the will. We can choose to live by either the flesh or the Spirit. So the moment you are tempted, turn to God and whisper a little prayer: "Lord, have mercy on me and fill me with Your Holy Spirit." If you have given in to the temptation, then start with confession. It is your choice. Choose wisely.

What has God already accomplished for every believer? How can every believer appropriate that?

How is crucifying the flesh a battle for the mind?

How is crucifying the flesh a crisis of the will?

What should you do when your mind starts drifting toward old flesh patterns?

Satan seems to know which button to push in tempting different people. What are your most vulnerable flesh patterns?

By *"death" and "life," Paul does not mean physical death and life but the death of sin and eternal life, which everyone who is mature in the Spirit and who has put to death the works of the flesh will attain. But we must also realize that this mortification of the deeds of the flesh comes through patience—not suddenly but step by step. At first they start to wilt in those who have been converted, but then, as they progress in their faith and become more dedicated, the deeds of the flesh not only wilt, they start to die out. But when they reach maturity to the point that there is no longer any trace in them of any sinful thought, word, or deed, then they may be reckoned to have completely mortified the deeds of the flesh.*

Origen (AD 184–253)

4

Defining the World
Zephaniah 1:14–18; 2:1–15

Key Point

The wisdom of this world is earthly, natural, and demonic.

Key Verse

Brothers and sisters, I could not address you as people who live by the Spirit but as people who are still worldly—mere infants in Christ.

1 Corinthians 3:1

Zephaniah preached the coming of the "great day of the LORD" (Zephaniah 1:14). God would be merciful to His people, but the world would be judged (see 3:8) and all the godless nations in it (see 2:1–15). The term "world" (Greek *kosmos*) basically means "order" or "system." *Kosmos* can mean the entire created universe (see Acts 17:24), the earth (see Mark 8:36) and frequently the world of humanity (see John 3:16, 19), which is under the dominion of sin. Consequently, "the world" is a term used to speak of the complex system of humanity apart from God. The institutions, structures, values, and mores of this world are primarily godless.

The moral character of this fallen world system is evil and its animosity toward God can be seen in what Jesus said to His disciples in John 15:18–19: "If the world hates you, keep in mind that it hated me first. If you belonged to the world, it would love you as its own. As it is, you do not belong to the world, but I have chosen you out of the world." As Christians, we live in this world but are not of this world. The wisdom of the world looks at the cross of Christ as foolishness and is antithetical to the wisdom of God (see 1 Corinthians 1:18–24). The nature of this world is evil because it is the domain of Satan's rule (see 1 John 5:19).

The true characteristics of the world are seen in 1 John 2:16: "For everything in the world—the lust of the flesh, the lust of the eyes, and the pride of life—comes not from the Father but from the world." The "lust of the flesh" is the sinful desires of our fallen human nature. The "lust of the eyes" relates to looking only on the outward appearance of people or things without seeing their real value. It is the love of beauty divorced from the love of goodness. Eve saw the forbidden fruit in the Garden of Eden as "pleasing to the eye" (Genesis 3:6). Achan said, "When I saw in the plunder a beautiful robe from Babylonia, two hundred shekels of silver and a bar of gold weighing fifty shekels, I coveted them and took them" (Joshua 7:21). David saw that Bathsheba "was very beautiful" (2 Samuel 11:2) and sinned grievously.

The Greek term for "boasting" describes those who make more of themselves than reality justifies. This boastful pride of life is what drives fallen humanity to exercise their own sovereign right to decide the shape of their lives. This attitude is not limited to the braggart. John indicates that it is the attitude of all those who live apart from God (see 1 John 2:16). These characteristics are not from the Father but from the world. If God is not included in who we are and what we do, then it is from the world. "Such 'wisdom' does not come down from heaven but is earthly, unspiritual, demonic" (James 3:15).

This worldly way of thinking is a product of the Fall. God created the world, and under His sovereign rule we were supposed to tend it. Everything God created is good, but now "we know that the whole creation has been groaning as in the pains of childbirth right up to the present time" (Romans 8:22).

What is the difference between being a good steward of the earth and shunning the world that hates you?

What is the meaning of the "world" in Scripture?

What is the difference between living in this world but not being of this world?

How would you describe a worldly person?

Do you think Christians should be concerned about the environment and about being good stewards of natural resources? Why or why not?

Paul also says, "The unspiritual man does not know the things which come from the Spirit of God." Contentious and proud wisdom is rightly described as earthly, unspiritual and devilish because as long as the soul seeks earthly glory it is deprived of spiritual grace and remains cut off from God. For now it thinks only what comes naturally to it since it originally fell. It is persuaded by the delusion of an evil spirit to do things which are wicked and harmful.

Bede (AD 673–735)

5

Overcoming the World

Nahum 1:1–15

Key Point

You know you have overcome the world when you look forward to a greater reward than the passing pleasures of this world.

Key Verses

Do not deceive yourselves. If any of you think you are wise by the standards of this age, you should become "fools" so that you may become wise. For the wisdom of this world is foolishness in God's sight.

1 Corinthians 3:18–19

Nineveh was a worldly city characterized by the godless nature of its people. Nahum communicated to its inhabitants that God was "slow to anger" (Nahum 1:3) and a refuge "for those who trust in him" (verse 7), but He would not leave the guilty unpunished (see verse 3). The Ninevites never overcame their worldliness and were doomed.

We also can let our affections be drawn to the world. For this reason we are warned, "Do not love the world or anything in the world. If anyone loves the world, love for the Father is not in them" (1 John 2:15). As Christians we are betrothed to Christ, but we are tempted to commit adultery with the world. "You adulterous people, don't you know that friendship with the world means enmity against God? Therefore, anyone who chooses to be a friend of the world becomes an enemy of God" (James 4:4).

The world seeks to weaken our love for Christ by appealing to our old nature, which desires to live according to the world's values. The temptation of the world is to satisfy our pleasures and not seek that which pleases God. The world system promotes self-sufficiency, but we have all the resources we need to withstand these threats. "For everyone born of God overcomes the world. This is the victory that has overcome the world, even our faith" (1 John 5:4).

In the first sentence of this verse, "overcomes" is in the present tense. This does not mean that believers never succumb to the temptation of the world but that victory (rather than defeat) generally characterizes their lives. In the second sentence, "has overcome" is in the past tense, indicating that the action is finished. This is consistent with the truth that when we came to Christ, we were joined to the One who could say, "Take heart! I have overcome the world" (John 16:33). Christ's triumph over the powers of sin belongs to every believer who is alive in Him.

"Who is it that overcomes the world? Only the one who believes that Jesus is the Son of God" (1 John 5:5). John switches back to the present tense, indicating an ongoing sense of overcoming—that is, the daily experience of our victory over the world because we are alive in Christ. When we placed our faith in Christ, we became overcomers, and we continue to live like overcomers when we continue to believe all that God says is true. "You, dear children, are from God and have overcome [false prophets], because the one who is in you is greater than the one who is in the world. . . . We are from God, and whoever knows God listens to us; but whoever is not from God does not listen to us" (1 John 4:4, 6).

Jesus said, "What good will it be for someone to gain the whole world, yet forfeits their soul? Or what can anyone give in exchange for their soul? For the Son of Man is going to come in his Father's glory with his angels, and then he will reward each person according to what they have done" (Matthew 16:26–27). You can store up treasures on earth or treasures in heaven. You know you have overcome the world when you look forward to a greater reward than the passing pleasures of this world.

Why was the Lord angry against Ninevah? How do you think He feels about America?

How does our love for the world weaken our love for Christ?

How is "overcoming the world" both a past and present action?

What worldly wisdom and treasures are most alluring to you? How long would you be happy and satisfied if you obtained them?

How can you know if you have overcome your love for the world?

Whoever loves the world by committing sin is revealed as an enemy of God, just as, on the other hand, one who affirms friendship with God by not sinning is a constant enemy of the world. Therefore, just as it is impossible to serve both God and mammon, so it is also impossible to be a friend of the world and of God at the same time.

Didymus the Blind (AD 313–398)

Kingdom Sovereignty

While I was conducting a Discipleship Counseling conference in Austria, a missionary couple from Africa asked if I could help their son. He had been seduced by a shaman's magical powers that he wanted for himself and had participated in some tribal rituals. Now he was under psychiatric care. When we met, there was a menacing look on his face that had a pretense of spiritual superiority. I said to him, "This is not about your authority and power." He immediately replied, "Yes, authority and power!" When he renounced that lie, I was able to lead him through the Steps to Freedom in Christ.

Another time, a woman was sharing her story when she suddenly went catatonic. Sensing the opposition, I calmly said, "Satan, you have no authority here." Then I said to her, "You can open your eyes now," and she did. Another individual was being spiritually harassed, and suddenly the enemy spoke through the person and said, "Who the [*expletive*] do you think you are?" I said, "I'm a child of God. You shut up." In both cases, the individuals finished the Steps to Freedom and were liberated in Christ.

By what power and authority do we have the right to do this kind of ministry? Who is qualified? There is little question that when it comes to Kingdom ministries, authority is *the* issue. So who has the right to rule?

Daily Readings

1. Authority and Power	Luke 10:17–23
2. The Authority of Christ	Matthew 28:16–20
3. The Conferring of Spiritual Authority	Ephesians 1:1–2:7
4. Qualifications for Spiritual Authority	Luke 9:10–62
5. The Limitations of Spiritual Authority	Acts 19:13–20

1

Authority and Power

Luke 10:17–23

Key Point

Our focus must be on the answer, who is Christ, and not the problem.

Key Verse

[Let us fix] our eyes on Jesus, the author and perfecter of faith.

Hebrews 12:2 NASB

When Jesus had called the Twelve together, he gave them power and authority to drive out all demons and to cure diseases" (Luke 9:1). Jesus sent these first twelve disciples out on a training mission to proclaim the kingdom of God. Then Jesus appointed seventy-two others and sent them out. "The seventy-two returned with joy and said, 'Lord, even the demons submit to us in your name'" (Luke 10:17). In proclaiming the kingdom of God, these missionaries were confronting the kingdom of darkness, and they discovered that demons were subject to them in the name of Jesus.

Satan had suffered another defeat at the hands of these itinerant missionaries because Jesus had given them authority and power over his demonic emissaries. They were successful in taking back some of the ground that Satan had captured. Jesus went on to say, "I have given you authority to trample on snakes and scorpions and to overcome all the power of the enemy; nothing will harm you" (verse 19). Snakes and scorpions are not our enemies; Jesus is alluding to Satan and his demonic hierarchy.

Subjection is a military term that means "to rank under." Authority is the right to rule, and power is the ability to rule. As believers, we have the right to rule over the kingdom of darkness because of our position in Christ. We also have the ability to rule because of the indwelling power of the Holy Spirit. Therefore, we should "be strong in the Lord and in his mighty power" (Ephesians 6:10).

It is critically important that we understand that the authority and power we possess in Christ are His power and authority, which are over the kingdom of darkness. We have the power and authority to do God's will, and nothing more. Every member of the Body of Christ has the same authority and power, because it is all based on our identity and position in Christ, which is the same for every believer. Satan can't do anything about your identity and position in Christ, but if he can deceive you into believing that it is not true or irrelevant, you will live as though it isn't.

Jesus must have found it necessary to put in perspective His disciples' enthusiasm about their authority over the kingdom of darkness. Flushed with victory, we can also easily lose our perspective and adopt a wrong focus. Remember that pride comes before a fall. Jesus wants us to know that demons are subject to us but that our joy comes from knowing Him. We are to rejoice that we are children of God. Our focus has to be on the answer and not the problem. This is a consistent issue in Christianity. You don't have to know the lie; you have to know the truth. Counselors get bogged down in a paralysis of analysis. All the analysis in the world doesn't set anyone free.

To maintain our victory, we must be Christ-centered, not demon-centered. In doing so, we cannot let the devil set the agenda. The devil has succeeded if he can get us to pay attention to him and what he is doing instead of fixing our eyes on Jesus and paying attention to what God is doing. We should never allow evil spirits to distract us from our devotion to Christ (see 2 Corinthians 11:3).

What did the disciples and the seventy-two others discover when they confronted the kingdom of darkness in the name of Christ?

What is the difference between authority and power?

What is the difference between kingdom power and authority and the governing authority given to human governments, parents, and teachers (see Romans 13:1)?

Do you believe that you have the same power and authority to do God's will that other more mature Christians, pastors, and missionaries have? Why or why not?

Why is it so important to know who you are in Christ? Which would benefit you more: finding out what is wrong about yourself or finding out what is right about being a child of God?

_____

_____

_____

The grace bestowed upon the holy apostles is worthy of all admiration. But the bountifulness of the Giver surpasses all praise and admiration. He gives them, as I said, His own glory. They receive authority over the evil spirits. They reduce to nothing the pride of the devil that was so highly exalted and arrogant. They render ineffectual the demon's wickedness. By the might and efficiency of the Holy Spirit, burning them as if they were on fire, they make the devil come forth with groans and weeping from those whom he had possessed.

Cyril of Alexandria (AD 376–444)

2

The Authority of Christ

Matthew 28:16–20

Key Point

All authority in heaven and on this earth has been given to Jesus.

Key Verse

Then the end will come, when he hands over the kingdom to God the Father after he has destroyed all dominion, authority and power.

1 Corinthians 15:24

Satan had succeeded in filling the heart of Judas to betray Christ (see John 13:2). It was to the remaining eleven disciples that Jesus gave the Great Commission. Jesus said to them, "Go and make disciples of all nations, baptizing them in the name of the Father and of the Son and of the Holy Spirit, and teaching them to obey everything I have commanded you. And surely I am with you always, to the very end of the age" (Matthew 28:19–20). Nothing could be more comforting than to know that God is with us no matter where we go and that He will be until the end of time.

There are only two criteria that must be fulfilled in order for the Great Commission to be accomplished. First, we must be empowered. That is why Jesus said to His disciples, "Do not leave Jerusalem, but wait for the gift my Father promised, which you have heard me speak about. . . . But you will receive power when the Holy Spirit comes on you; and you will be my witnesses in Jerusalem, and in all Judea and Samaria, and to the ends of the earth" (Acts 1:4, 8). All those who are filled with the Holy Spirit are empowered to do His will.

Second, we must have the authority to do God's will. The Great Commission can only be understood in light of Jesus' previous words to His disciples: "All authority in heaven and on earth has been given to me. Therefore go and make disciples of all nations" (Matthew 28:18–19). One cannot delegate responsibility without authority. Jesus never appealed to His own authority until He had to delegate responsibility, even though that authority had been recognized. "The crowds were amazed at his teaching, because he taught as one who had authority, and not as their teachers of the law" (Matthew 7:28–29). If all authority has been given to Jesus, then Satan has no authority over any believer. Tragically, many believers don't know their position in Christ, so evil spirits easily intimidate them.

Satan wants to be feared, because he wants to be worshiped. If we consider his attributes to be equal to God's attributes, we will believe we are caught in a battle between two equal but opposite powers. Any Christian who believes that is defeated. God is omnipresent, omnipotent, and omniscient, and Satan is disarmed (see Colossians 2:15). Children of God are spiritually alive and seated with Christ in the heavenlies. We are joint heirs with Jesus and have the authority to continue His work on earth.

When evil forces confront us, we can say with confidence that we are children of God and that the evil one cannot harm us (see 1 John 5:18). Satan will try to intimidate us, and we can easily allow that to happen if we don't know the truth. He wants us to respond to his attacks in fear, because then he is in control. If we respond in fear, we are operating in the flesh, which is on his level. The fear of anything other than God is mutually exclusive with faith in God. We have lost control if we start shouting and screaming. The authority we have in Christ does not increase with volume. We don't shout out the devil! We just take our place in Christ and calmly say, "I'm a child of God, and you can't touch me!"

What is the practical significance of knowing that all authority has been given to Jesus?

How successful will we be in fulfilling the Great Commission if we are ignorant of our position in Christ and live according to the flesh?

Why does Satan want people to fear him? What are the consequences if we do?

Why do you think most believers are more afraid of Satan and demons than they are of God?

Are parents who shout, scream, and threaten their children exercising their God-given authority, or are they undermining it because they are living according to the flesh? How is this any different from exercising our authority over the kingdom of darkness?

"Jesus approached them and said, 'All authority in heaven and earth has been given to Me.'" This authority was given to one who had just been crucified, buried in a tomb, laid dead and afterwards had arisen. Authority was given to Him in both heaven and earth so that He who once reigned in heaven might also reign on earth through the faith of His believers.

Jerome (AD 347–420)

3

The Conferring of Spiritual Authority and Power

Ephesians 1:1–2:7

Key Point

The last thing the devil wants you to know is who you are in Christ, which is why the Holy Spirit bears witness with your Spirit that you are a child of God.

Key Verse

And God raised us up with Christ and seated us with him in the heavenly realms in Christ Jesus.

Ephesians 2:6

Praise be to the God and Father of our Lord Jesus Christ, who has blessed us in the heavenly realms with every spiritual blessing in Christ" (Ephesians 1:3). In Christ we were chosen (see verse 4) and "in Him we have redemption" (see verse 7). Our hope lies in Christ (see verse 12), and we "were marked in him with a seal" (verse 13).

The problem is that we don't always recognize or understand this remarkable inheritance that we have been given in Christ. As Paul expresses for all believers, "I pray that the eyes of your heart may be enlightened in order that you may know the hope to which he has called you, the riches of his glorious inheritance in his holy people, and his incomparably great power [*dunameos*] for us who believe. That power [*energeian*] is the same as the mighty [*kratous*] strength [*ischuos*] he exerted when he raised Christ from the dead" (verses 18–20).

Behind Christ's authority is the same power that raised Him from the dead and seated Him at the Father's right hand. That power source is so dynamic that Paul uses four different Greek words to describe it (see italicized words in brackets in quote above). Behind the resurrection of the Lord Jesus Christ lies the mightiest work of power recorded in the Bible. The same power that raised Jesus from the dead and defeated Satan is available to us as believers. When we don't understand and appropriate our spiritual heritage, we don't experience the freedom and the fruitfulness that is intrinsic to our position in Christ. To carry out our delegated responsibility, we have to know the authority we have in Christ and the power of the Holy Spirit who indwells us.

The scope of Christ's authority is "far above all rule and authority, power and dominion, and every name that is invoked, not only in the present age but also in the one to come" (verse 21). We share this same authority because we are seated with Christ in the heavenly realms (see 2:4–7). We are not *being* made alive in Christ; we *have been* made alive in Christ. We are not *being* raised up with Christ; we *have been* raised up with Christ. We are right now together with Christ. The throne of God is the ultimate authority of the universe, and it is from this position of authority that we carry on our delegated Kingdom responsibilities.

Before Christ, we were dead in our transgressions and sins. We "followed the ways of this world and of the ruler of the kingdom of the air, the spirit who is now at work in those who are disobedient" (verse 2). But now we have received "the incomparable riches of his grace, expressed in his kindness to us in Christ Jesus" (verse 7). "His intent was that now, through the church, the manifold wisdom of God should be made known to the rulers and authorities in the heavenly realms, according to his eternal purpose that he accomplished in Christ Jesus our Lord" (3:10–11). The last thing the devil wants you to know is who you are in Christ, because he can't intimidate a child of God who knows they are forgiven, made alive, empowered, and authorized to make disciples.

What is the rich inheritance that we have in Christ?

What is the scope of the power and authority that believers have in Christ?

What is the significance of our being seated with Christ in the heavenlies?

Do you think it is prideful to know your identity and position in Christ or essential for your victory? Do prideful people know who they are in Christ?

From the beginning of this VICTORY SERIES, knowing who we are "in Christ" has been a major emphasis. How has that impacted you in terms of knowing who you are, how to live, and how to stand firm in your faith?

_____

_____

_____

What Paul is saying then is: If you believe that Christ is risen from the dead, believe also that you too have risen with Him. If you believe that He sits at the Father's right hand in heaven, believe that your place too is amid not earthly but heavenly things.

Origen (AD 184–253)

4

Qualifications for Spiritual Authority

Luke 9:10–62

Key Point

There are eight kingdom-killing attitudes that will render us ineffective.

Key Verse

I begged your disciples to drive [a demon] out, but they could not.

Luke 9:40

Although Jesus gave the twelve disciples power and authority over demons and sent them out to proclaim the kingdom of God (see Luke 9:1), they could not free a father's son from demonic control (see verses 37–43). Jesus had to reveal to them several kingdom-killing attitudes. The first attitude concerned their sense of self-sufficiency. When Jesus withdrew with the disciples to the town of Bethsaida, the crowd followed them (see verse 10). It grew late, and the disciples showed concern for the people, so Jesus said, "You give them something to eat" (verse 13). The disciples made a common error when given a humanly impossible task. They looked at their own limited resources and concluded it couldn't be done.

Jesus took what they had and multiplied it. There was so much food left over that each disciple had a basket of his own (see verses 11–17), but they gained no insight from the experience (see Mark 6:45–52). When they struggled against the storm at sea, the Lord intended to pass them by (see verse 48). Jesus intends to pass by the self-sufficient. If we want to row against the storms of life, He will let us row until our arms fall off, or we can call on the name of the Lord and depend on Him.

The second attitude Jesus warned them about was being ashamed of Him and His words (see Luke 9:26). It is easy to imagine that Jesus could be ashamed of us, but how can any person who knows the truth be ashamed of Jesus? If we are ashamed of Jesus, He will be ashamed of us when He comes again.

The third kingdom-killing attitude was unbelief (see verses 37–43). The disciples were ineffective in helping the demon-possessed boy because they really didn't believe. Jesus implies some moral impurity on their part with His stinging rebuke, "You unbelieving and perverse generation" (Luke 9:41). The power we have in Christ is only effective when we repent and believe.

The fourth attitude that made the twelve disciples ineffective was pride (see Luke 9:46–48). They were arguing among themselves as to who was the greatest. According to Jesus, the greatest are those who humble themselves and come to God with childlike faith. Humble people are confident in God and put no confidence in the flesh (see Philippians 3:3).

The fifth kingdom-killing attitude was possessiveness (see Luke 9:49–50). We may be driving different cars in the kingdom of God, but we are all getting our gas from the same station. No one person or ministry is superior to another, and what God has given us we should freely share with others.

The sixth attitude the disciples displayed was the wrong spirit (see verses 51–56). What kind of spirit requests permission to use the power of God to destroy? It may be human nature to retaliate against those who reject us, but it is not God's nature. If it were, we would all be doomed.

The seventh kingdom-killing attitude was a false confidence (see verses 57–58). It is better to have a few followers who have counted the cost and will endure to the end than to have a crowd who will leave before the task is done.

The eighth kingdom-killing attitude was lame excuses (see verses 59–62). Jesus tells us, "No one who puts a hand to the plow and looks back is fit for service in the kingdom of God" (verse 62).

In Luke 9:37–43, why couldn't the disciples free the father's son from demonic control?

Which of the eight kingdom-killing attitudes is most prevalent in the Church today?

How effective can we expect our churches to be if those attitudes are present? (Keep in mind that those attitudes were present in our Lord's inner circle.)

Which of those eight attitudes would most concern you for your own sake and for the sake of your ministry? Why?

These attitudes will keep you from being effective in ministry. However, is that the only negative consequence (i.e. do they also leave us vulnerable)?

_____

_____

_____

The passion and lust of pride attacked some of the holy apostles. The mere argument about who of them was the greatest is the mark of an ambitious person, eager to stand at the head of the rest. Christ, who did not sleep, knows how to deliver. He saw this thought in the disciple's mind, springing up, in the words of Scripture, like some bitter plant. He saw the weeds, the work of the wicked sower. . . . In what way does the Physician of souls amputate pride's passion? How does He deliver the beloved disciple from being prey of the enemy and from a thing hateful to God and man? He took a child and set him beside them.

Cyril of Alexandria (AD 376–444)

5

The Limitations of
Spiritual Authority

Acts 19:13–20

Key Point

Believers only have the spiritual authority to do God's will.

Key Verse

Apart from me you can do nothing.

John 15:5

If something seems to be working, opportunists start jumping on board. Such was the case of some Jews who apparently thought they could perform exorcisms through a magical formula or by simply using the name of Jesus. The seven sons of Sceva (a Jewish high priest) were doing this (see Acts 19:13–14). To their surprise, they got beaten up and run out of the house by a demonized man (see verse 16).

The demon said he knew Jesus and Paul, but not the seven sons of Sceva. The demon didn't beat them up. The demonized man did. He was able to overpower them because of the adrenaline rush the evil spirit had stimulated within him. It is the same phenomenon that gives people extraordinary strength to lift objects to save people, although in such instances their strength comes from a different spirit.

If a demonized person questions who we are, all we have to say is, "I am a child of God and you can't touch me" (see 1 John 5:18). All believers, young and old, have the same authority and power over demons, although mature saints may know better how to exercise it. People can get hurt when they misuse or fail to understand the power and authority they have in Christ. We only have the authority to do God's will. We are operating according to our old nature when we act independently of God. In the flesh we are no match for evil spirits. We will suffer defeat if we operate independently of God, but demons are no match for those who depend on God!

The news of the seven sons getting beat up by a demonized person created fear among the people, but fortunately they turned to Jesus and held His name in honor (see Acts 19:17). Many of the believers openly confessed their evil deeds (see verse 18). Those who were practicing sorcery brought the tools of their practice and burned them (see verse 19). The word of the Lord spread rapidly and grew in power (see verse 20). One of the major thrusts of Early Church evangelism was to free people from demonic influences. That may likely be the case again before the second coming of Christ.

It is human nature to see something work and borrow the method instead of understanding the message behind the method. There are no programs, rituals, or formulas that can set anybody free. Who sets people free is Christ, and what sets people free is their response to God in repentance and faith. If God is in it, almost any program will work. It God isn't in it, then no program will work, no matter how biblical it may appear. But if God is in it, then a good program and strategy will bear more fruit than a bad program or strategy.

A missionary couple once tried to help a demonized man but ended up getting attacked themselves. They explained, "We said out loud that we are children of God and the evil one can't touch us, but it didn't work." The problem was that they said it defensively in fear and not in confident faith with the assurance that they were indeed children of God. Scripture is a not a Band-Aid to be placed on sore spots. The couple could have said to the demonized man in confidence, "I know who I am in Christ, and I know the authority and power I have in Him is greater than the disarmed and deceiving spirit that is tormenting you."

Why were the sons of Sceva unable to free the man from the demon?

_____

_____

_____

What does this story reveal about our limitations in exerting spiritual authority?

_____

_____

_____

How can just doing something or just saying something "in the name of Jesus" be ineffective? What would make it effective?

_____

_____

_____

What is wrong with formulaic or ritualistic Christianity? How has that affected you?

_____

_____

_____

What would you do if some spirit manifested in your room at night?

_____

_____

_____

Therefore, since "Satan disguises himself as an angel of light," Satan has no fear of covering his ministers as well with the same false appearance. . . . Because they called upon the name of Christ and the apostles not out of belief in them but to put them to the test, they were rightly condemned for the cunning deceitfulness, not only by God but also by the demons themselves.

Bede (AD 673–735)

The Armor of God (Part 1)

One day in Portiuncula [a small church located in central Italy] while at prayer alone in his cell, St. Francis saw a vision of the whole house surrounded and besieged by devils. They were like a great army surrounding the place, but none of them could gain entrance to the house. The brothers were so disciplined and devoted in their lives of sanctity that the devils were frustrated without a host upon whom they might find a way in.

It happened, in the days soon after Francis's vision, that one of the brothers became offended by another and he began to think in his heart of ways to revenge the slight. While the scheming brother was devising vengeful plans, entertaining wicked thoughts, the devil, finding an open door, entered Portiuncula upon his back.

Francis, the watchful shepherd of his flock, saw that the wolf had entered, intending to devour his little sheep. At once, Francis called the brother to him and asked him to disclose the hatred that had caused this disturbance in his house. The brother, frightened that Francis knew the content of his heart, disclosed to him all of the venom and malice that consumed him, acknowledging his fault and begging humbly for forgiveness.

Loving his sheep as does his Father, the shepherd soon absolved the brother, and immediately, at that moment, before his very face, Francis saw the devil flee from his presence. The brother returned to the flock and the wolf was gone from the house.[1]

—Paul Sabatier, *The Road to Assisi*

Daily Readings

1. Putting on the Armor	Ephesians 6:10–20
2. The Belt of Truth	John 17:13–19
3. The Breastplate of Righteousness	Acts 24:10–16
4. The Shoes of Peace	Romans 16:17–20
5. The Shield of Faith	Psalm 7:10–16

1

Putting on the Armor
Ephesians 6:10–20

Key Point

Christ is our sanctuary.

Key Verse

The night is nearly over; the day is almost here. So let us put aside the deeds of darkness and put on the armor of light.

Romans 13:12

Satan's first objective is to blind the mind of the unbelieving (see 2 Corinthians 4:3–4). When that fails, his next objective is to deceive, tempt, and accuse believers. Satan's aim is to "prove" that Christianity doesn't work, that God's Word isn't true, and that nothing really happened when we were born again. Because our struggle is against spiritual forces of wickedness, we need to know how to protect ourselves.

Westerners have a strange reaction to the notion that unseen demons are present, but so are germs, which they can't see either. Approximately two hundred years ago we didn't even know that germs existed. Doctors didn't wear surgical masks, sterilize their equipment, scrub before surgery, or use antibiotics. Consequently, a lot of people got sick, and the average person died before they were fifty. Now that we know there are germs, what should we do? If we become germ-oriented and start looking for them, we will become hypochondriacs. The appropriate response is to live a healthy life. Our immune system will protect us if we get enough sleep, exercise regularly, and eat a healthy diet.

There are demons in this world! So we must live a righteous life. Yet if that is all we have to do, why do we need to even know about them? For the same reason we need to know there are germs. If there were no evil spirits, there would be no need to put on the armor of God, to take every thought captive to the obedience of Christ, or to stand firm and resist the enemy. Ignorance and passive resistance will leave a lot of people in bondage, sick, and dying (physically and spiritually).

When we put on the armor of God, we are putting on the Lord Jesus Christ. "So let us put aside the deeds of darkness and put on the armor of light. Let us behave decently, as in the daytime, not in carousing and drunkenness, not in sexual immorality and debauchery, not in dissension and jealousy. Rather, clothe yourselves with the Lord Jesus Christ, and do not think about how to gratify the desires of the flesh" (Romans 13:12–14).

We are only vulnerable when we live according to the flesh, which is why we are to make no provision for the flesh. Satan has nothing on Christ (see John 14:30), and to the extent that we put on Christ, the evil one cannot touch us (see 1 John 5:18). There is no physical sanctuary or place where we are spiritually protected, and there is no time when it is safe to take off the armor of God. Our only sanctuary is our identity and position in Christ (see Ephesians 6:10).

Putting on the armor of God requires active participation on our part. We cannot passively take our place in Christ. As Paul describes the armor of God, he admonishes us to "be strong" (Ephesians 6:10), "put on" (verse 11), "take [our] stand" (verse 11), "stand firm" (verse 14), "take up" (verse 16), "take" (verse 17), "pray" (verse 18) and "be alert" (verse 18). "Therefore put on the full armor of God, so that when the day of evil comes, you may be able to stand your ground" (verse 13). The purpose for armor is to stop penetration, and we become vulnerable if we do not assume our responsibility to stand firm in our faith.

Why should our focus be on good health and righteous living as opposed to looking for germs and demons?

_____

_____

_____

Why do we need to know that there are evil spirits seeking our ruin?

_____

_____

_____

What is the danger of passive resistance or pleading ignorance?

_____

_____

_____

_____

How can you practically "put on the full armor of God"?

_____

_____

_____

_____

Where are you most vulnerable (i.e., deceived and believing lies, tempted and sinning, accused and feeling condemned)? What is your defense?

_____

_____

_____

We have often said that Christ is wisdom, righteousness, holiness, truth and all the other virtues. Therefore anyone who has acquired these has put on Christ. For if all these are Christ, then the person who has them must of necessity have Christ as well. Whoever has them will not bother about the flesh.

Origen (AD 184–253)

2

The Belt of Truth

John 17:13–19

Key Point

Knowing the truth is our first line of defense against the father of lies.

Key Verse

Don't be deceived, my dear brothers and sisters. Every good and perfect gift is from above, coming down from the Father of the heavenly lights, who does not change like shifting shadows. He chose to give us birth through the word of truth.

James 1:16–18

Jesus was about to ascend into heaven and leave behind His beloved disciples, whom He had commissioned to go into all the world where the devil was prowling around seeking someone to devour. Notice the first concern of our Lord in His high priestly prayer: "My prayer is not that you take them out of the world but that you protect them from the evil one. They are not of the world, even as I am not of it. Sanctify them by the truth; your word is truth" (John 17:15–17).

Deception is the devil's greatest weapon, and God's Word is our first line of defense, which is why the belt of truth is the first piece of God's armor. Lying is the most common defense mechanism employed by unbelievers and possibly the greatest sin of believers. Those who have something to hide will seek to cover it up, and in so doing they will play right into the hands of Satan, who is the father of lies. We will stay in bondage as long as we continue to believe his lies. Some don't want the truth to be known, because their deeds are evil and they don't want them exposed (see John 3:20).

The first step in any recovery program is to face the truth and acknowledge our need for God, who alone has the power to overcome our sin. Those who turn to Christ find their sanctuary in Him, because Jesus is the truth (see John 14:6), the Holy Spirit is the Spirit of Truth (see John 14:17), He will lead us into all truth (see John 16:13), and that truth will set us free (see John 8:32).

If the devil tempted you, you would know it. If he accused you, you would know it. But if Satan deceived you, you wouldn't know it, because if you did, you would no longer be deceived. That is why deception is the major tool of the devil. The fact that even good people can be deceived is evident in the sinless life of Eve before the Fall. She was deceived and believed a lie (see Genesis 3:1–6). Satan's strategy was deception in the Garden of Eden, and will be until his final demise. "And the great dragon was thrown down, the serpent of old who is called the devil and Satan, who deceives the whole world" (Revelation 12:9 NASB). Spiritual deception will likely intensify in the end times with the coming of the false prophet and the Antichrist.

We don't overcome the father of lies through human reason or scientific research. We overcome the deceiver by divine revelation. We are admonished to walk in the light (see 1 John 1:7) and to speak the truth in love (see Ephesians 4:25). The only thing we as Christians ever have to admit to is the truth. We never have to be afraid of the truth, for it is a liberating friend. Therefore, "Trust in the LORD with all your heart and lean not on your own understanding; in all your ways submit to him, and he will make your paths straight. Do not be wise in your own eyes; fear the LORD and shun evil. This will bring health to your body and nourishment to your bones" (Proverbs 3:5–8).

How do lying and covering up play into the hands of Satan?

_____

_____

_____

Why is deception a main tool that the enemy uses to get us to fall?

_____

_____

_____

Why is admitting the truth the first step in any recovery program?

_____

_____

_____

How can you recognize the lie if you don't know the truth? What does that suggest about the need to know God's Word?

_____

_____

_____

Would people know you as an honest person who always tells the truth and lives in the light? Why or why not?

_____

_____

_____

Christ does not wish for the apostles to be set free of human affairs or to be rid of life in the body when they have not yet finished the course of their apostleship or distinguished themselves by the virtues of a godly life. Rather, His desire is to see them live their lives in the company of people in the world and guide the footsteps of those whe are His to a state of life well pleasing to God. After they have done this, then at last, with the glory they have achieved, they will be carried into the heavenly city and dwell with the company of the holy angels.

Cyril of Alexandria (AD 376–444)

3

The Breastplate of Righteousness

Acts 24:10–16

Key Point

We are clothed with Christ's righteousness.

Key Verse

And the scripture was fulfilled that says, "Abraham believed God, and it was credited to him as righteousness," and he was called God's friend.

James 2:23

When we put on Christ at salvation, we were justified before a Holy God (see Romans 5:1). It is not our righteousness that saved us, but Christ's righteousness (see 1 Corinthians 1:30). When we put on the armor of God, we are putting on the breastplate of righteousness, which is our defense against Satan's accusations.

Every believer has struggled with condemning thoughts, because Satan is the accuser of the brethren "who accuses them before our God day and night" (Revelation 12:10). When he reminds God of your past, you can remind him of his future. However, it is better to respond with Paul, "Who will bring any charge against those whom God has chosen? It is God who justifies" (Romans 8:33). The breastplate of righteousness is the Lord's righteousness bestowed on us. This righteousness is imputed at salvation. "Imputed righteousness" means that something that belongs to one person is put on the account of another.

God also imparts His righteousness within us. The Puritans called this "imparted righteousness." Because we have become partakers of God's righteous nature, we can live a holy life. "For it is God who works in you to will and to act in order to fulfill his good purpose" (Philippians 2:13). Even though we stand in a righteous position in Christ, we should not commit or excuse any deeds of unrighteousness. We are saints who still have the capacity to sin, and we will if we believe a lie or choose to live according to the old nature. Putting on the armor of light means that we walk in the light as God is in the light (see 1 John 1:6–7).

John wrote, "If we claim to be without sin, we deceive ourselves and the truth is not in us" (1 John 1:8). Walking in the light is not sinless perfection; it is simply agreeing with God. It is essentially the same as confession, which is taken from the Greek *homologeo*, which means "to acknowledge or agree."

In Paul's defense before Felix, he appealed to his orthodox beliefs and then said, "So I strive always to keep my conscience clear before God and man" (Acts 24:16). That is good advice for all of us. When we realize that we have done something wrong, we confess it. We don't have to ask for forgiveness, because we are already forgiven. Any residual guilt is a false guilt or Satan's accusations, because "there is now no condemnation for those who are in Christ Jesus" (Romans 8:1).

You can walk in the light because you are already forgiven. You are the righteousness of God in Christ (see 2 Corinthians 5:21). Your relationship with God and your eternal destiny are not at stake when you sin, but your daily victory is. Your confession of sin clears the way for the fruitful expression of righteousness in your daily life. "My dear children, I write this to you so that you will not sin. But if anybody does sin, we have an advocate with the Father—Jesus Christ, the Righteous One. He is the atoning sacrifice for our sins, and not only for ours but also for the sins of the whole world" (1 John 2:1–2).

What does it mean to put on the breastplate of righteousness?

What is the difference between imputed and imparted righteousness?

Why is it so important to keep close accounts with God in our daily walk?

How should you respond if condemning thoughts plague you?

Who should you fear if your righteousness is a pretense? Why?

....

....

....

One who has put on a sturdy breastplate is difficult to wound. Especially well-protected are those essential parts of the body upon which life depends. So put on the breastplate. Strap it together by iron rings and insert the hooks in their place. One protected by such a breastplate of righteousness will not be like a vulnerable stag that receives the arrow in his liver. He will not lapse into rage or lust. Rather he will be protected, having a clean heart, having God as the fashioner of his breastplate, since He fashions the whole armor for every one of the saints.

Jerome (AD 347–420)

4

The Shoes of Peace
Romans 16:17–20

Key Point

Godly people are peacemakers who sow seeds of unity while the devil sows seeds of discord.

Key Verse

Let us therefore make every effort to do what leads to peace and to mutual edification.

Romans 14:19

There are a lot of divisive elements in this world, so Paul cautions us to watch out for them. Divisive people are not serving our Lord Jesus Christ. "By smooth talk and flattery they deceive the minds of naïve people" (Romans 16:18). Paul wrote in Titus 3:10–11, "Warn a divisive person once, and then warn them a second time. After that, have nothing to do with them. You may be sure that such people are warped and sinful; they are self-condemned." Divisive people stand in stark contrast to true believers. Jesus tells us, "Blessed are the peacemakers, for they will be called children of God" (Matthew 5:9).

In John 17:21, Jesus prays that we would all be one. In Ephesians 4:3, Paul admonishes us to "make every effort to keep the unity of the Spirit through the bond of peace." If we are going to keep the unity of the Spirit, then it must somehow be present with us already. Therefore, the basis for unity is not our common physical heritage, nor is it our religious traditions. The basis for our unity is our common spiritual heritage. Every believer is a child of God. We are brothers and sisters in Christ, and we ought to relate to one another as such.

When we receive Christ, we are united with the Prince of Peace. We already have positional peace with God (see Romans 5:1), but the peace of Christ must rule in our hearts. That happens when we let the Word of Christ richly dwell within us (see Colossians 3:15–16). The shoes of peace, as armor of God, become our protection against the divisive schemes of the devil when we act as peacemakers among believers.

A tree that is split in half soon dies, but a tree that is pruned bears more fruit. Jesus prunes, but the devil divides—and it takes little effort to divide a fellowship. All you have to do is start a whisper campaign, spread a few lies, and accuse someone falsely. The book of Proverbs has a lot to say about malicious speech and gossip: "A gossip betrays a confidence, but a trustworthy person keeps a secret" (11:13); "A perverse person stirs up dissension, and a gossip separates close friends" (16:28); "Without wood a fire goes out; without gossip a quarrel dies down" (26:20).

Satan will try to divide a person's mind, because a double-minded person is unstable in all his or her ways (see James 1:8). He will try to divide a home, because a house divided against itself cannot stand (see Mark 3:25). He will try to divide the body of Christ, because united we stand but divided we fall. Unless we are alert, we will be like blindfolded warriors who don't know who our enemy is. We will strike out at ourselves and at each other.

Such is the divisive work of Satan and his false prophets. However, we have the promise that "the God of peace will soon crush Satan under [our] feet" (Romans 16:20). If we want to be peacemakers, we should "not let any unwholesome talk come out of [our] mouths, but only what is helpful for building others up according to their needs, that it may benefit those who listen. And [we should] not grieve the Holy Spirit of God, with whom [we] were sealed for the day of redemption" (Ephesians 4:29–30).

A heretic is one who causes divisions. How should the church deal with such people?

What is the basis for unity among believers in Christ?

How does the devil seek to divide us?

What divisions have you seen in your own thinking? In your family? In your church?

How can you make a conscious effort to be a better peacemaker?

_____

_____

_____

Your footwear is not put on in order that you may walk around foolishly but to accomplish the course of the gospel. In this way you will receive the prophetic blessing: "How lovely on the mountains are the feet of him who brings good news."

Theodoret of Cyr (AD 393–457)

5

The Shield of Faith

Psalm 7:10–16

Key Point

God is our shield and protector, which we appropriate by faith.

Key Verse

Every word of God is flawless; he is a shield to those who take refuge in him.

Proverbs 30:5

As a young shepherd, David had protected his sheep from lions (see 1 Samuel 17:34–35). Now, as an adult, enemies surrounded David, so he took refuge in the Lord. He knew in his heart that God was the only One who could save him. David wrote, "My shield is God Most High, who saves the upright in heart" (Psalm 7:10). As a New Testament believer, you also have to "take up the shield of faith, with which you can extinguish all the flaming arrows of the evil one" (Ephesians 6:16). The Greek word for shield (*thureos*) conveys the idea of a large shield. It was a shield that the infantry would hide behind when the enemy shot their arrows.

These "flaming arrows" are nothing more than smoldering lies, burning accusations, and fiery temptations bombarding our minds. Whenever we discern a deceiving, accusing, or tempting thought, we must not pay attention to it. We take every thought captive and make it obedient to Christ (see 2 Corinthians 10:5). We let it bounce off the shield of faith. This is what Jesus did when the devil tempted Him—He simply quoted Scripture. Satan's flaming arrows are extinguished by the truth. Every time we memorize a Bible verse, listen to a sermon, or participate in a Bible study, we increase our knowledge of God and enlarge our shield of faith. "Every word of God is flawless; he is a shield to those who take refuge in him" (Proverbs 30:5).

Recall that putting on the armor of God is essentially putting on the Lord Jesus Christ. He is our sanctuary, and He is our shield, which we appropriate by faith. The object of our faith is our shield, because faith has no validity without an object. For instance, we may believe that the police are there to protect us, as well as fire departments. What will happen if we hear a burglar or sense a fire in the house and believe the police and firefighters will save us, but never make the call? The fact that we believe we can call on them is not what provides us with protection. Police and fire departments provide physical protection if we make the call. "Everyone who calls on the name of the Lord will be saved" (Acts 2:21), so when you are under mental assault, make the call and choose the truth. Say, "Lord, I need Your protection and I choose to believe the truth."

Psalm 91 describes the sanctuary we have in God. "Whoever dwells in the shelter of the Most High will rest in the shadow of the Almighty" (verse 1). He will deliver us from the fowler's snare (see verse 3) and cover us with His shield (see verse 4). "You will not fear the terror of night, nor the arrow that flies by day. . . . For he will command his angels concerning you to guard you in all your ways" (verses 5, 11).

Satan knew the spiritual significance of this last verse when he tempted Jesus in the wilderness (see Matthew 4:6), but Jesus would not be tempted to put God to the test. We are protected when we do God's will, not Satan's will. "'Because he loves me,' says the LORD, 'I will rescue him; I will protect him, for he acknowledges my name'" (Psalm 91:14).

Is God our shield, or is what we believe our shield, or both?

What are the "flaming arrows" of the enemy?

Who is our sanctuary? How can we take refuge in Him?

What should you do if you suddenly discerned that you had been paying attention to a deceiving spirit (see 1 Timothy 4:1)?

How does it help you to know that you can call on the name of the Lord inwardly, since He knows your thoughts and intentions?

By "his darts" Paul means both temptations and perverse desires. He calls them fiery because that is the nature of the appetite. Faith is capable of commanding hosts of demons. How much more is faith capable of ordering the passions of the soul?

John Chrysostom (AD 347–407)

The Armor of God (Part 2)

A woman at Eisenach [a town in Germany] lay very sick, having endured horrible paroxysms [a fit or attack], which no physician was able to cure, for it was directly the work of the devil. She had had swoonings and four paroxysms, each lasting three or four hours. Her hands and her feet bent in the form of a horn; she was chill and cold; her tongue was rough and dry; her body was much swollen.

She, seeing [Martin] Luther, who came to visit her, was much rejoiced thereat, raised herself up, and said: "Ah! My loving father in Christ, I have a heavy burden upon me, pray to God for me," and so fell down in her bed again. Whereupon Luther sighed and said: "God rebuke thee, Satan, and command thee that thou suffer this, his divine creature, to be at peace."

Then turning himself towards the standers-by, he said, "She is plagued of the devil in the body, but the soul is safe, and shall be preserved; therefore let us give thanks to God, and pray for her"; and so they all prayed aloud the Lord's Prayer. After which, Luther concluded with these words: "Lord God, heavenly Father! Who hast commanded us to pray for the sick, we beseech thee, through Jesus Christ, thy only Son, that thou wouldst deliver this soul, which, together with her body, thou hast purchased and redeemed from the power of sin, of death, and of the devil." Whereupon the sick woman said, "Amen."

The night following she took rest, and the next day was graciously delivered from her disease and sickness.[1]

—Martin Luther

Daily Readings

1. The Helmet of Salvation	Psalm 27:1–14
2. The Sword of the Spirit	Psalm 119:89–112
3. Praying with Perseverance for All the Saints	Luke 18:1–8
4. Praying with Authority	1 Kings 18:16–38
5. Binding and Loosing	Matthew 16:13–23

1

The Helmet of Salvation
Psalm 27:1–14

Key Point

The helmet of salvation is the guardian of spiritual life.

Key Verse

Yet to all who did receive him, to those who believed in his name, he gave the right to become children of God—children born not of natural descent, nor of human decision or a husband's will, but born of God.

John 1:12–13

In the metaphor of God's armor, the helmet secures coverage of the most critical part of our anatomy—our head—where spiritual battles are won or lost. A blow to any other part of our anatomy is painful, wounding, and crippling, but a blow to the head is often fatal. Death is the absence of salvation. The temptation is to doubt our salvation when we come under spiritual attack. The mental assault is fairly predictable. *How can you even think you are a Christian given the way you act and feel? God doesn't love you. You don't believe this Christian stuff, do you?* We can stand firm knowing that our salvation is not based on our good works but on the good works of Christ. We are children of God by the grace of God, and nothing can separate us from His love (see Romans 8:35).

Christian warriors wear the helmet of salvation in the sense that they are possessors of deliverance who are clothed and armed in the victory of Jesus Christ. Because we are joined to the Lord Jesus Christ, the devil has no legitimate claim on us, and thus there is no reason to fear him. David said, "The Lord is my light and my salvation—whom shall I fear? The Lord is the stronghold of my life—of whom shall I be afraid?" (Psalm 27:1). "For God did not appoint us to suffer wrath but to receive salvation through our Lord Jesus Christ" (1 Thessalonians 5:9).

Unlike Satan, the Lord does not intrude where He is not invited, which is why it is up to us to receive Him in at salvation (see John 1:12). The Lord will never disown us or leave us. Even if we strayed away from God, we would still be His children. Our salvation is not based on our ability to hang on to God but His ability to hang on to us. "I give them eternal life, and they shall never perish; no one can snatch them out of my hand. My Father, who has given them to me, is greater than all; no one can snatch them out of my Father's hand" (John 10:28–30).

Satan cannot do anything about our relationship with God, but if he can get us to doubt our salvation, we will struggle in our daily life. Victorious Christians know "that neither death nor life, neither angels nor demons, neither the present nor the future, nor any powers, neither height nor depth, nor anything else in all creation, will be able to separate us from the love of God that is in Christ Jesus our Lord" (Romans 8:38–39).

A grateful mother once wrote, "Add one more person to the list of those set free from bondage. Yesterday, my pastor led me through the Steps to Freedom in Christ, and I am free. My four-year-old daughter was hearing growling in her closet. I led her through a simpler version of the Steps, and now she is free. We have talked at great length about who she is in Christ and all that Satan is not. Sometimes I hear her in her room saying, 'I belong to Jesus, and you have to leave me alone.' She's not having problems anymore. Praise the Lord."

Why is the helmet of salvation a matter of life and death?

How secure are people if they doubt their salvation?

What can separate Christians from the love of God? Who can snatch a Christian away from God?

How confident are you in your salvation? Who is it dependent on?

How secure are you if you doubt your salvation? How can you stand against the intrusive thoughts that question your salvation?

It is Christ indeed who is the author of salvation. He is our head. He descended to us and redeemed us by His own mystery. It is He indeed who guards the heads of the faithful. Therefore He is the "helmet of salvation." He is the Word by which the adverse powers are overcome and taken captive. . . . Christ, who is the Word of God, was sent to overcome all corruption and wickedness and even death itself.

Gaius Marius Victorinus (c. fourth century AD)

2

The Sword of the Spirit
Psalm 119:89–112

Key Point

Believers go on the offensive with the sword of the Spirit.

Key Verse

Amid disquieting dreams in the night, when deep sleep falls on people, fear and trembling seized me and made all my bones shake. A spirit glided past my face, and the hair on my body stood on end.

Job 4:13–15

God's Word is eternal (see Psalm 119:89), a lamp to our feet and a light to our path (see verse 105). The Word of God is the only offensive weapon in the armor of God. It is the "sword of the Spirit" (Ephesians 6:17). Paul uses *rhema* instead of *logos* for "word," because the Greek word *rhema* carries the idea of proclamation. Our defense against the direct attacks from the evil one is to speak aloud God's truth. In addition to thinking and believing God's Word, we need to speak it because Satan is not omniscient and he doesn't perfectly know what we are thinking. By observing us, he can know reasonably well what we are thinking, just as any student of human behavior can.

If you are paying attention to a deceiving spirit (see 1 Timothy 4:1), he is putting thoughts into your mind and will know by how you behave whether you buy his lies. It isn't hard for Satan to know what you are thinking if he has given you the thought. You are ascribing too much power to Satan if you think he can perfectly read your mind and know the future. Occult practitioners claim to be able to read minds (or influence them) or predict the future. However, Satan doesn't know perfectly either. We should never ascribe the divine attributes of God to Satan.

It is not uncommon for people to come under a spiritual attack at night (see Job 4:12–16). The usual experience is an intense feeling of fear and the inability to speak or move. It may feel like a pressure on our chest or something grabbing our throat. We can easily resolve such spiritual attacks by submitting to God first, and then resisting the devil (see James 4:7). We can always silently and inwardly call on the name of the Lord, because God knows the thoughts and attitudes of our hearts (see Hebrews 4:12). As soon as we acknowledge God, He will enable us to resist the devil. All we have to say is "Jesus" and the evil spirit will flee, but we have to verbally express it. Trying to respond physically wouldn't work, because we don't wage war as the world does (see 2 Corinthians 10:3–4). Spiritual battles have to be won spiritually.

"If you declare with your mouth, 'Jesus is Lord,' and believe in your heart that God raised him from the dead, you will be saved. For it is with your heart that you believe and are justified, and it is with your mouth that you profess your faith and are saved" (Romans 10:9–10). You know your own thoughts and God also knows them, so why does verbal confession result in salvation? Paul is saying that saving faith is not complete until the will is exercised, but he is also implying the need for the god of this world to hear our commitment.

Jesus fasted for forty days, and then the Holy Spirit led Him into the wilderness to be tempted. He was on the verge of starvation, alone and isolated. Nobody could be more vulnerable. He answered the tempter by speaking God's Word (see Matthew 4:1–11). Christians face their greatest temptations when they are alone, but they also won't be embarrassed by verbally rebuking the devil in the name of Jesus.

Why is it important for believers to speak the truth and not just think it?

Why is the scriptural order of submitting to God first before resisting the devil so essential?

Why do we need to confess with our mouth that Jesus is Lord?

When are you most vulnerable spiritually?

Why is it far more effective to verbally resist the devil when you are by yourself and being tempted? (Try it—it works!)

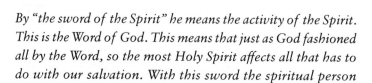

By "the sword of the Spirit" he means the activity of the Spirit. This is the Word of God. This means that just as God fashioned all by the Word, so the most Holy Spirit affects all that has to do with our salvation. With this sword the spiritual person rebukes the devil, and the devil flees.

Theodoret of Cyr (AD 393–457)

3

Praying with Perseverance for All the Saints

Luke 18:1–8

Key Point

Prayer doesn't precede a greater work; it is our greater work.

Key Verses

Be diligent in these matters; give yourself wholly to them, so that everyone may see your progress. Watch your life and doctrine closely. Persevere in them, because if you do, you will save both yourself and your hearers.

1 Timothy 4:15–16

Paul's discussion on the armor of God concludes with this admonition: "Pray in the Spirit on all occasions with all kinds of prayers and requests. With this in mind, be alert and always keep on praying for all the Lord's people [saints]" (Ephesians 6:18). Spiritual warfare is fought on our knees. Praying on "all occasions" means we are to pray when we feel like it and when we don't feel like it. If we declare our dependence on God, we will pray often and be ready all the time. The preeminence of prayer needs to be settled in our minds. Prayer doesn't precede a greater work of God. Prayer *is* our greater work.

Prayer has preceded every great movement of God. Pentecost was preceded by prayer, as were the Great Awakenings in America. There has never been an outpouring of the divine Spirit from God without a previous outpouring of the human spirit toward God through prayer. Any prayer that the Holy Spirit prompts you to pray is a prayer that God the Father will always answer.

The Holy Spirit will prompt us to intercede for the needs of others. Such prompting may come in the middle of the night or at any time of the day. We may never know the trouble another believer is experiencing, but the Holy Spirit does. So when the Lord puts someone on your mind, stop whatever you're doing and lift him or her up in prayer. Ask God to place a hedge of protection around that person. Be persistent in prayer until you sense the peace of God.

The Holy Spirit may also prompt us to pray for those who are in bondage. We have the spiritual authority in Christ to stand against Satan and his attacks. When the disciples were unsuccessful in driving out a demon in a boy, the Lord said, "This kind can come out only by prayer" (Mark 9:29). The disciples may have tried to drive out the demon by copying what they saw Jesus do, but they didn't have the same degree of dependence on their heavenly Father that Jesus did, nor the same degree of faith.

Jesus told the parable of the unjust judge so that His disciples would learn to be persistent in prayer (see Luke 18:1–8). The widow only wanted justice against her adversary, and she wasn't going to stop petitioning the judge until she got it. Her persistence finally won over the judge, who gave her justice. If a judge who doesn't care for that which is right or wrong is compelled by persistence to deal justly with a helpless individual, certainly we can expect God to answer prayer. He will not put us off, and He will quickly answer our cry for justice concerning our adversaries.

Before the Lord returns, there will be a coming apostasy. During this time of spiritual decline and persecution, the Lord asks whether He will find faith on the earth (see Luke 18:8). Presumably, He means the kind of faith that perseveres in prayer and never wavers under fire. Prayer is not conquering God's reluctance but laying hold of God's willingness. Asking is the rule of the kingdom, which demonstrates our dependence on God.

Why is prayer a necessary first step in any endeavor—including waging spiritual battles against the enemy?

When and how should we pray for others?

Why is perseverance in prayer so important for our lives and ministry?

What should you do when the Holy Spirit brings someone's name to your mind?

Why does God want you to personally be alert and praying?

This means that we should not say or utter particular words or recite them in our prayers as though they were premeditated or written down. We are to "pray in the spirit" at "all times." Let your deep affections enter into your praying. The inner spirit— that is, the inner man—is making his prayer with intense desire. He is praying all the time, so that even when he is not praying aloud he is still praying in the spirit.

Gaius Marius Victorinus (c. fourth century AD)

4

Praying with Authority

1 Kings 18:16–38

Key Point

Prayer is discerning God's will and then speaking the Word of God with boldness.

Key Verses

"You unbelieving and perverse generation," Jesus replied, "how long shall I stay with you? How long shall I put up with you? Bring the boy here to me." Jesus rebuked the demon, and it came out of the boy, and he was healed at that moment.

Matthew 17:17–18

James said, "Elijah was a human being, even as we are. He prayed earnestly that it would not rain, and it did not rain on the land for three and a half years. Again he prayed, and the heavens gave rain, and the earth produced its crops" (James 5:17–18). Elijah was a prophet of God, but he was a mortal just like us. We have the same spiritual authority as Elijah, because of our position in Christ.

The key to Elijah's success is found in 1 Kings 18:36–38. He desired that God be known in Israel and that the hearts of the people would be turned back to Him. His confidence and faith in God were so great that he could see the answer to prayer before there was any visible evidence (see verses 41–45). He was sure of what he hoped for and certain of what he did not see, which is the epitome of faith (see Hebrews 11:1).

Every believer has the spiritual authority to do God's will and carry on the ministry of Christ. Jesus summarized His ministry when He read Isaiah 61:1–2 in the synagogue and applied it to Himself: "The Spirit of the Lord is on me, because he has anointed me to preach good news to the poor. He has sent me to proclaim freedom for the prisoners and recovery of sight for the blind, to set the oppressed free" (Luke 4:18). In this present Church Age, God works through the prayers and faith of His children whom He has commissioned to make disciples of all nations. We have authority over Satan and his demons who have blinded the minds of the unbelieving (see 2 Corinthians 4:4) and captivated many people to do his will (see 2 Timothy 2:26).

Satan's power has been broken (see Hebrews 2:14–15; Colossians 2:15), but he will not turn loose anything he thinks he can keep. Jesus came to undo the works of Satan (see 1 John 3:8), and it is part of our calling to recapture lost ground. We need to stand firm in our faith and pray with the authority delegated to us by the Lord Jesus Christ. We are not trying to enlist God in our service—through prayer, we are joining God in His service. Praying with authority is not expressing our will to God but discerning God's will and claiming the answer with confidence.

"This is the confidence we have in approaching God: that if we ask anything according to his will, he hears us. And if we know that he hears us—whatever we ask—we know that we have what we asked of him" (1 John 5:14–15). We have the right to claim by faith the property that Satan has his hands on but which rightfully belongs to God. We need to persevere in faith until Satan turns loose those for whom God has directed us to pray. The evil one will hold on to his captives until we take our place in Christ and demand that he release them in the name of Jesus!

Consider how the Early Church prayed when they experienced opposition: "Now, Lord, consider their threats and enable your servants to speak your word with great boldness. Stretch out your hand to heal and perform miraculous signs and wonders through the name of your holy servant Jesus" (Acts 4:29–30).

What was the key to Elijah's success over the prophets of Baal?

Under what situations do we, like Elijah, have the ability to pray with authority?

How did God answer the believers' prayer in Acts 4:29–30?

What is keeping you from praying boldly and with confidence?

Are you prepared to have your life and daily routines disrupted by the filling of God's Holy Spirit? Why or why not?

God heard their prayer and manifested this by shaking the place. For "when they had prayed," it is said, "the place was shaken." . . . And God did this both to make it more fearsome and to lead them to courage. After those threatening conditions, they gained increased boldness. Since this was the beginning of their ministry and they had prayed for a sensible sign for their persuasion, great was the encouragement they received. In fact, they had no means of proving that He was risen except by miraculous signs. Thus it was not only their own assurance that they sought but also that they might not be put to shame, that they might speak with boldness. "The place was shaken," and that made them all the more unshaken.

John Chrysostom (AD 347–407)

5

Binding and Loosing

Matthew 16:13–23

Key Point

God has given the keys of the Kingdom to those who deny themselves, pick up their cross daily, and follow Jesus.

Key Verse

For I have come down from heaven not to do my will but to do the will of him who sent me.

John 6:38

God revealed to Peter that Jesus was "the Messiah, the Son of the living God" (Matthew 16:16). A short time later, Peter found himself speaking for the devil. Jesus rebuked him, saying, "Get behind me, Satan! You are a stumbling block to me; you do not have in mind the concerns of God, but merely human concerns" (verse 23).

Jesus' rebuke seems severe, but the fact that He identified Satan as the source of Peter's words was precise and appropriate. The devil's aim is to promote self-interest as the chief end of humankind. Satan is called the prince of this world because self-interest rules this world. He is called the accuser because he does not believe that we have a higher motive than self-service. Satan's creed sounds like this: "Save yourself at all costs. Sacrifice duty to self-interest, the cause of Christ to personal convenience. All people are selfish at heart and have their price. Some may hold out longer than others, but in the end people choose their own will over the will of God."

God has given the keys of the Kingdom to those who deny themselves, pick up their cross daily, and follow Jesus. Whatever they bind on earth will be bound in heaven, and whatever they loose on earth will be loosed in heaven (see Matthew 16:19). A similar passage can be found in Matthew 18:18, but in verses 19–20, Jesus adds, "I tell you that if two of you on earth agree about anything they ask for, it will be done for them by my Father in heaven. For where two or three gather in my name, there am I with them."

Three points need to be noted. First, because truth sets people free, the keys of the Kingdom may mean the keys of knowledge (see Luke 11:52). Second, both passages on binding and loosing are difficult to translate. Following the rules of Greek grammar, both passages can be translated, "Whatever you bind on earth shall have been bound in heaven, and whatever you loose on earth shall have been loosed in heaven" (Matthew 16:19 NASB).

The same Greek language structure is found in John 20:23: "If you forgive anyone's sins, their sins are forgiven; if you do not forgive them, they are not forgiven." That passage could also be translated, "If you forgive the sins of any, their sins have been forgiven them; if you retain the sins of any, they have been retained" (John 20:23 NASB). Notice the subtle differences between the two translations. Linguistically, they can be translated either way, but the New American Standard Bible translation is to be preferred. Most theologians agree that the Church does not have the power and right to bind, loose, and forgive whomever it wishes.

Third, what the two or three gathered together in Jesus' name are agreeing on is God's will. The ideas to bind, loose, and forgive originated in heaven, not in the independent mind of humanity. God is able to communicate in such a way that discerning Christians have the keys to the

Kingdom. They are announcing what God has ordained. Everything that is true and lasting originates in heaven.

Why did Jesus react so strongly to Peter when he said that Christ would not suffer and die?

_____

_____

_____

How does Satan work to promote self-interest among believers?

_____

_____

_____

Where does the authority to bind, loose, and forgive originate? How do we minister that authority?

_____

_____

_____

_____

What confidence do you gain when you find agreement with others in prayer?

_____

_____

_____

_____

Should you find two or three others who would agree with you in prayer, or should you find two or three others who would join you in agreeing with God in prayer? Explain.

_____

_____

_____

_____

For Christ is a rock which is never disturbed or worn away. Therefore Peter gladly received his name from Christ to signify the established and unshaken faith of the church. . . . The devil is the gateway of death who always hastens to stir up against the holy church calamities and temptations and persecutions. But the faith of the apostle, which was founded on the rock of Christ, abides always unconquered and unshaken. And the very keys of the kingdom of the heavens have been handed down so that one whom he has bound on earth has been bound in heaven, and one whom He has set free on earth he has also set free in heaven.

Epiphanius Scholasticus (c. sixth century AD)

Leader's Tips

The following are some guidelines for leaders to follow when using the VICTORY SERIES studies with a small group. Generally, the ideal size for a group is between 10 and 20 people, which is small enough for meaningful fellowship but large enough for dynamic group interaction. It is typically best to stop opening up the group to members after the second session and invite them to join the next study after the six weeks are complete.

Structuring Your Time Together

For best results, ensure that all participants have a copy of the book. They should be encouraged to read the material and consider the questions and applications on their own before the group session. If participants have to miss a meeting, they should keep abreast of the study on their own. The group session reinforces what they learned and offers the valuable perspectives of others. Learning best takes place in the context of committed relationships, so do more than just share answers. Take the time to care and share with one another. You might want to use the first week to distribute material and give everyone a chance to tell others who they are.

If you discussed just one topic a week, it would take several years to finish the VICTORY SERIES. If you did five a week, it is possible to complete the whole series in 48 weeks. All the books in the series were written with a six-week study in mind. However, each group is different and each will have to discover its own pace. If too many participants come unprepared, you may have to read, or at least summarize, the text before discussing the questions and applications.

It would be great if this series was used for a church staff or Bible study at work and could be done one topic at a time, five days a week. However, most study groups will likely be meeting weekly. It is best to start with a time of sharing and prayer for one another. Start with the text or Bible passage for each topic and move to the discussion questions and application. Take time at the end to summarize what has been covered, and dismiss in prayer.

Group Dynamics

Getting a group of people actively involved in discussing critical issues of the Christian life is very rewarding. Not only does group interaction help to create interest, stimulate thinking, and encourage effective learning, but it is also vital for building quality relationships within the group. Only as people begin to share their thoughts and feelings will they begin to build bonds of friendship and support.

It is important to set some guidelines at the beginning of the study, as follows:

- There are no wrong questions.
- Everyone should feel free to share his or her ideas without recrimination.
- Focus on the issues and not on personalities.
- Try not to dominate the discussions or let others do so.
- Personal issues shared in the group must remain in the group.
- Avoid gossiping about others in or outside the group.
- Side issues should be diverted to the end of the class for those who wish to linger and discuss them further.
- Above all, help each other grow in Christ.

Some may find it difficult to share with others, and that is okay. It takes time to develop trust in any group. A leader can create a more open and sharing atmosphere by being appropriately vulnerable himself or herself. A good leader doesn't have all the answers and doesn't need to for this study. Some questions raised are extremely difficult to answer and have been puzzled over for years by educated believers. We will never have all the answers to every question in this age, but that does not preclude discussion over eternal matters. Hopefully, it will cause some to dig deeper.

Leading the Group

The following tips can be helpful in making group interaction a positive learning opportunity for everyone:

- When a question or comment is raised that is off the subject, suggest that you will bring it up again at the end of the class if anyone is still interested.

- When someone talks too much, direct a few questions specifically to other people, making sure not to put any shy people on the spot. Talk privately with the "dominator" and ask for cooperation in helping to draw out the quieter group members.

- Hopefully the participants have already written their answers to the discussion questions and will share that when asked. If most haven't come prepared, give them some time to personally reflect on what has been written and the questions asked.

- If someone asks a question that you don't know how to answer, admit it and move on. If the question calls for insight about personal experience, invite group members to comment. If the question requires specialized knowledge, offer to look for an answer before the next session. (Make sure to follow up the next session.)

- When group members disagree with you or each other, remind them that it is possible to disagree without becoming disagreeable. To help clarify the issues while maintaining a climate of mutual acceptance, encourage those on opposite sides to restate what they have heard the other person(s) saying about the issue. Then invite each side to evaluate how accurately they feel their position was presented. Ask group members to identify as many points as possible related to the topic on which both sides agree, and then lead the group in examining

151

other Scriptures related to the topic, looking for common ground that they can all accept.

- Finally, urge group members to keep an open heart and mind and a willingness to continue loving one another while learning more about the topic at hand.

If the disagreement involves an issue on which your church has stated a position, be sure that stance is clearly and positively presented. This should be done not to squelch dissent but to ensure that there is no confusion over where your church stands.

Notes

Session Two: Good and Evil Spirits

Chapter 3: The Ministry of Angels

1. Billy Graham, *Angels: God's Secret Agents* (Waco, TX: Word Books, 1986), p. 3.

Session Three: Overcoming the Opposition

1. Theodore Roosevelt, from the speech "Citizenship in a Republic," delivered at the Sorbonne, in Paris, France, on April 23, 1910.

Session Five: The Armor of God (Part 1)

1. Paul Sabatier, *The Road to Assisi: The Essential Biography of St. Francis* (Brewster, MA: Paraclete Press, 2003), p. 167.

Session Six: The Armor of God (Part 2)

1. Martin Luther, *The Table Talk of Martin Luther*, ed. Thomas S. Kepler (Grand Rapids, MI: Baker Book House, 1952), pp. 292–293.

Victory Series Scope and Sequence Overview

The VICTORY SERIES is composed of eight studies that create a comprehensive discipleship course. Each study builds on the previous one and provides six sessions of material. These can be used by an individual or in a small group setting. There are leader's tips at the back of each study for those leading a small group.

The following scope and sequence overview gives a brief summary of the content of each of the eight studies in the VICTORY SERIES. Some studies also include articles related to the content of that study.

The Victory Series

Study 1 God's Story for You: Discover the Person God Created You to Be

Session One: The Story of Creation
Session Two: The Story of the Fall
Session Three: The Story of Salvation
Session Four: The Story of God's Sanctification
Session Five: The Story of God's Transforming Power
Session Six: The Story of God

Study 2 Your New Identity: A Transforming Union With God

Session One: A New Life "in Christ"
Session Two: A New Understanding of God's Character
Session Three: A New Understanding of God's Nature
Session Four: A New Relationship With God
Session Five: A New Humanity
Session Six: A New Beginning

Study 3 Your Foundation in Christ: Live by the Power of the Spirit

---

Session One: Liberating Truth
Session Two: The Nature of Faith
Session Three: Living Boldly
Session Four: Godly Relationships
Session Five: Freedom of Forgiveness
Session Six: Living by the Spirit

Study 4 Renewing Your Mind: Become More Like Christ

Session One: Being Transformed
Session Two: Living Under Grace
Session Three: Overcoming Anger
Session Four: Overcoming Anxiety
Session Five: Overcoming Depression
Session Six: Overcoming Losses

Study 5 Growing in Christ: Deepen Your Relationship With Jesus

---

Session One: Spiritual Discernment
Session Two: Spiritual Gifts
Session Three: Growing Through Committed Relationships
Session Four: Overcoming Sexual Bondage
Session Five: Overcoming Chemical Addiction
Session Six: Suffering for Righteousness' Sake

Study 6 Your Life in Christ: Walk in Freedom by Faith

Session One: God's Will
Session Two: Faith Appraisal (Part 1)
Session Three: Faith Appraisal (Part 2)
Session Four: Spiritual Leadership
Session Five: Discipleship Counseling
Session Six: The Kingdom of God

Study 7   Your Authority in Christ: Overcome Strongholds in Your Life

---

Session One: The Origin of Evil
Session Two: Good and Evil Spirits
Session Three: Overcoming the Opposition
Session Four: Kingdom Sovereignty
Session Five: The Armor of God (Part 1)
Session Six: The Armor of God (Part 2)

Study 8   Your Ultimate Victory: Stand Strong in the Faith

Session One: The Battle for Our Minds
Session Two: The Lure of Knowledge and Power
Session Three: Overcoming Temptation
Session Four: Overcoming Accusation
Session Five: Overcoming Deception
Session Six: Degrees of Spiritual Vulnerability

Books and Resources

Dr. Neil T. Anderson

Core Material

Victory Over the Darkness with study guide, audiobook, and DVD. With over 1,300,000 copies in print, this core book explains who you are in Christ, how to walk by faith in the power of the Holy Spirit, how to be transformed by the renewing of your mind, how to experience emotional freedom, and how to relate to one another in Christ.

The Bondage Breaker with study guide, audiobook, and DVD. With over 1,300,000 copies in print, this book explains spiritual warfare, what our protection is, ways that we are vulnerable, and how we can live a liberated life in Christ.

Breaking Through to Spiritual Maturity. This curriculum teaches the basic message of Freedom in Christ Ministries.

Discipleship Counseling with DVD. This book combines the concepts of discipleship and counseling and teaches the practical integration of theology and psychology for helping Christians resolve their personal and spiritual conflicts through repentance and faith in God.

Steps to Freedom in Christ and interactive video. This discipleship counseling tool helps Christians resolve their personal and spiritual conflicts through genuine repentance and faith in God.

Restored. This book is an expansion of the *Steps to Freedom in Christ*, and offers more explanation and illustrations.

Walking in Freedom. This book is a 21-day devotional that we use for follow-up after leading someone through the Steps to Freedom.

Freedom in Christ is a discipleship course for Sunday school classes and small groups. The course comes with a teacher's guide, a student guide, and a DVD covering 12 lessons and the Steps to Freedom in Christ. This course is designed to enable new and stagnant believers to resolve personal and spiritual conflicts and be established alive and free in Christ.

The Bondage Breaker DVD Experience is also a discipleship course for Sunday school classes and small groups. It is similar to the one above, but the lessons are 15 minutes instead of 30 minutes.

The Daily Discipler. This practical systematic theology is a culmination of all of Dr. Anderson's books covering the major doctrines of the Christian faith and the problems Christians face. It is a five-day-per-week, one-year study that will thoroughly ground believers in their faith.

Specialized Books

The Bondage Breaker, the Next Step. This book has several testimonies of people finding their freedom from all kinds of problems, with commentary by Dr. Anderson. It is an important learning tool for encouragers.

Overcoming Addictive Behavior, with Mike Quarles. This book explores the path to addiction and how a Christian can overcome addictive behaviors.

Overcoming Depression, with Joanne Anderson. This book explores the nature of depression, which is a body, soul, and spirit problem and presents a wholistic answer for overcoming this "common cold" of mental illness.

Liberating Prayer. This book helps believers understand the confusion in their minds when it comes time to pray, and why listening in prayer may be more important than talking.

Daily in Christ, with Joanne Anderson. This popular daily devotional is also being used by thousands of Internet subscribers every day.

Who I Am in Christ. In 36 short chapters, this book describes who you are in Christ and how He meets your deepest needs.

Freedom from Addiction, with Mike and Julia Quarles. Using Mike's testimony, this book explains the nature of chemical addictions and how to overcome them in Christ.

One Day at a Time, with Mike and Julia Quarles. This devotional helps those who struggle with addictive behaviors and explains how to discover the grace of God on a daily basis.

Freedom from Fear, with Rich Miller. This book explains anxiety disorders and how to overcome them.

Setting Your Church Free, with Charles Mylander. This book offers guidelines and encouragement for resolving seemingly impossible corporate conflicts in the church and also provides leaders with a primary means for church growth—releasing the power of God in the church.

Setting Your Marriage Free, with Dr. Charles Mylander. This book explains God's divine plan for marriage and the steps that couples can take to resolve their difficulties.

Christ-Centered Therapy, with Dr. Terry and Julie Zuehlke. This is a textbook explaining the practical integration of theology and psychology for professional counselors.

Getting Anger Under Control, with Rich Miller. This book explains the basis for anger and how to control it.

Grace that Breaks the Chains, with Rich Miller and Paul Travis. This book explains legalism and how to overcome it.

Winning the Battle Within. This book shares God's standards for sexual conduct, the path to sexual addiction, and how to overcome sexual strongholds.

The Path to Reconciliation. God has given the church the ministry of reconciliation. This book explains what that is and how it can be accomplished.

Rough Road to Freedom. This is a book of Dr. Anderson's memoirs.

For more information, contact Freedom In Christ Ministries at the following:

Canada: freedominchrist@sasktel.net or www.ficm.ca

India: isactara@gmail.com

Switzerland: info@freiheitinchristus.ch or www.freiheitinchristus.ch

United Kingdom: info@ficm.org.uk or www.ficm.org.uk

United States: info@ficm.org or www.ficm.org

International: www.ficminternational.org

Dr. Anderson: www.discipleshipcounsel.com

Index

Notes

Notes

Notes

Notes

Notes

Notes

Notes

Notes

Dr. Neil T. Anderson was formerly the chairman of the Practical Theology Department at Talbot School of Theology. In 1989, he founded Freedom in Christ Ministries, which now has staff and offices in various countries around the world. He is currently on the Freedom in Christ Ministries International Board, which oversees this global ministry. For more information about Dr. Anderson and his ministry, visit his website at www.ficminternational.org.

Also From
Neil T. Anderson

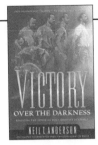

This bestselling landmark book gives you practical, productive ways to discover who you are in Christ. When you realize the power of your true identity, you can shed the burdens of your past, stand against evil influences, and become the person Christ empowers you to be.

Victory Over the Darkness

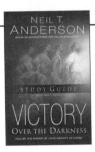

Great for small group or individual use, these thought-provoking personal reflection questions and applications for each chapter of *Victory Over the Darkness* will help readers grow in the strength and truth of their powerful identity in Jesus Christ.

Victory Over the Darkness Study Guide